THE
BEWL VALLEY
IRONWORKS

THE
BEWL VALLEY IRONWORKS
KENT

c. 1300 – 1730

DAVID CROSSLEY

THE ROYAL ARCHAEOLOGICAL INSTITUTE

Royal Archaeological Institute Monographs
Editor: M. J. Swanton

Published by the Royal Archaeological Institute
with the aid of a grant from
The Department of the Environment

ISBN 0 903986 03 5

PRINTED IN GREAT BRITAIN BY W. S. MANEY AND SON LTD   LEEDS   ENGLAND

CONTENTS

LIST OF ILLUSTRATIONS

ACKNOWLEDGEMENTS

The author wishes to acknowledge help from the following: The Department of the Environment for financing the excavation and the Society for Post-Medieval Archaeology for administering the grant; Mrs C. Hussey and the late Mr Christopher Hussey for permission to excavate on Scotney estate; their agents, Messrs Langridge and Freeman; the Medway Water Board; Mr and Mrs G. D. Veitch, of Bewl Bridge Farm, Miss Bevan of Copens, and Mrs Parsons of Upper Hazelhurst for assistance and access; Tonbridge Rural District Council, the Weald Iron Research Group and the Nuffield Foundation for assistance with equipment; the volunteers, too numerous to mention individually, but especially the supervisors, Frank Andrews, Denis Ashurst, Faith Cleverdon, John Fearon, Jeremy Haslam, Max Lyne and Lynn Willies; Margaret Browne for site surveys and for drawing the maps, Mr W. F. Beswick and Mr D. Butler for work on conservation of finds; Elizabeth Crossley, Ian Goodall, Jeremy Haslam, Sheila Jacobs and Dick Whinney for drawing plans and finds; Dr R. F. Tylecote for advice and assistance over the whole period of excavation and Mr S. E. Rigold for comments on pottery and on timber construction; and all those who have assisted with specialist help, mentioned in the course of this report. The material from the excavation will be deposited at Maidstone Museum.

The Institute is indebted to the Metals Society for a grant towards the cost of the plates in this paper.

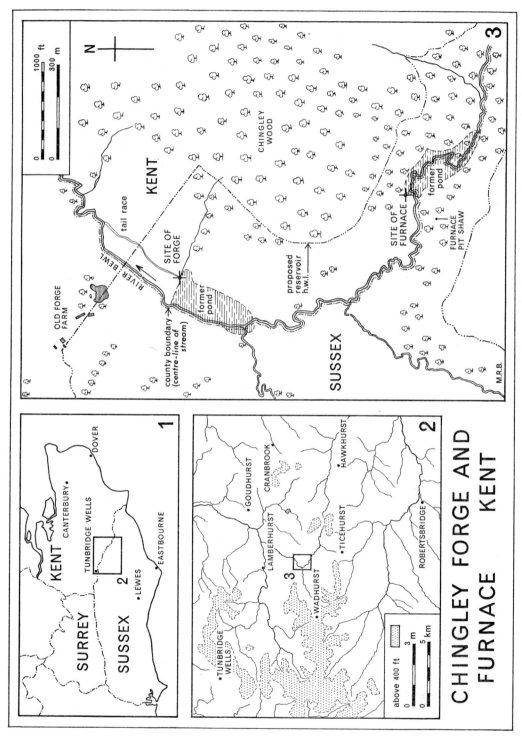

Fig. 1. The Bewl Valley: location (derived from the Ordnance Survey Map of 1909)

I   The Sites and their Surroundings

The river Bewl (Fig. 1) is a feeder for the Teise, itself a tributary of the Medway, and forms the boundary between Kent and Sussex south of Lamberhurst. It flows westwards into the reservoir area from its source north of Ticehurst, and before flooding took place[1] curved north round Chingley Wood, whose high thickly-timbered ground stretches north-east towards the main Lamberhurst-Robertsbridge road. The furnace site stood at the foot of the wood where the valley is narrow and steep sided, allowing the dam to be short and the supply-pond compact. Before clearance for the reservoir much of this part of the valley bottom was thickly overgrown with old coppice; and to the west the timber grew unevenly around the mine-pits of Furnace Pit Shaw, where the nodular ironstones occur in the outcrop of the Wadhurst clay.[2] Chingley Wood, on the other hand, while clearly once partly coppiced, now has considerable cover of old-established deciduous timber.

To the north, the valley opens into more level cleared ground, and the Bewl is joined from the west by two streams, the southerly un-named, flowing from Holbeanwood, the other the Hook River, whose tributaries rise to the east of Wadhurst. Immediately below this second confluence a flat water-meadow indicated the site of the former pond for Chingley Forge (Fig. 1:3). The dam had once stood half-way along this field, but in 1968 its line was barely visible, and the site of the forge was only indicated by the position of its tail-race. This could be seen as a ditch lined by alders and willows along the eastern side of the field whose western edge was marked by the Bewl itself. After its junction with the tail-race north of the reservoir dam, the river then flows to Bewl Bridge, where it is crossed by the turnpike road, and to Scotney Castle, whose moat it feeds, to join the Teise a mile to the east of Lamberhurst.

It is unlikely that the valley had changed in appearance since the abandonment of the forge early in the eighteenth century, apart from the creation of nineteenth-century valley-bottom boundaries; there is little evidence that the main field-pattern on the slopes had altered greatly since the original assarting, which left woodland, copse and uncleared belts between fields. While certain substantial farms on the western skyline such as Beaumans and Beales Barn have been developed over the period, the main valley has been left virtually without settlement between Bewl Bridge, to the north, and the sixteenth-century Dunster's Mill House, now being moved from its original site 700 yards east of the furnace. The only exception to this was Old Forge Farm, a now-demolished mid-seventeenth-century timber-framed house (Fig. 1:3) discussed below (p. 41), and contemporary although not definitely associated with the last use of the forge.

---

[1] Construction of the dam began in 1973, and while impounding may not be complete at the time this report is published a description based on the planned high-water mark of the reservoir will be more useful for the future reader.

[2] The strata within the Wadhurst clay are shown to be highly variable by boreholes made in preparation for the reservoir. See E. R. Shepherd-Thorn et al., *Geology of the Country round Tenterden* (London, 1966), esp. pp. 50–1 (bore no. 6, 1961–2, N.G.R. TQ 684335).

II   The Documentary Evidence

During its medieval period of use the forge was probably part of the manor of Chingley. The boundary between Chingley and Scotney lands appears to have run along the Bewl, as it did in the sixteenth century, and excavation suggested that before the valley was completely dammed across for the late sixteenth-century forge, the river's course ran on the western, or Scotney, side of the site (p. 14 and Fig. 2).[1]

There are two documentary references indicating medieval ironworking on Chingley manor. The first is not dated, but has been suggested to belong to the reign of Edward I;[2] this, one of the Ministers' Accounts for Boxley Abbey, shows that iron worth 53 shillings was due from Chingley manor to the Abbot. A date of *c.* 1300 would correspond with pottery found on the forge site. The second indication comes in six Ministers' Accounts dated between 1340 and 1354.[3] These make it clear that an ironworks was in operation on the demesne, with references to payments to smiths and for carriage of iron. Although none of these can be proved to relate to the site under consideration, a thorough exploration of the valley has not shown any alternative. Other material for the period, Rentals and Surveys, and Court Rolls, contain no useful references.

Skeletal evidence for the chronology of ownership and operation in the sixteenth and seventeenth centuries was set out by Straker and Schubert,[4] and while more material has now come to light, the picture has not greatly altered. The first important question, the date of the building of Chingley Furnace, is still obscure, for the first firm reference is the entry in the Robertsbridge Steelworks accounts to the supply of plates from Chingley furnace in 1565.[5] The *Valor Ecclesiasticus* of 1535 had made no mention of ironworks,[6] nor do the Ministers' Accounts for the period 1539–46. The omission from the *Valor* may mean anything or nothing, as its recording of details is far from consistent, but the Accounts record numbers of cottages and farms, and silence here suggests that the forge was still out of use and the furnace not yet begun.[7] Chingley manor passed through several hands; Thomas Vycary, the King's surgeon and his son William were appointed bailiffs of Boxley lands in October 1543,[8] although some, not including Chingley, had been granted to Sir Thomas Wyatt in 1540.[9] In 1544 Thomas Colepepper

---

[1] It would be misleading to state that the site was certainly part of Chingley by 1300, for Boxley Abbey was acquiring land to add to the manor all through the period (see *Calendar of Kent Feet of Fines*, Kent Arch. Soc. Records Branch 15 (1956), 177; *V.C.H. Kent*, II, 154). It is unfortunate that no useful material has survived for Scotney before its acquisition by John Darell in 1418, on his marriage to the niece of Archbishop Chicheley; see E. Hussey, 'Scotney Castle', *Archaeologia Cantiana*, 17 (1887), 39.

[2] P.R.O. SC6/1251/2. The compiler of *List and Index: Ministers' Accounts*, put this as 'temp. Edward I', *Appendix* (1965), p. 519, a judgement which there is no good reason to challenge.

[3] P.R.O., SC6/889/2–6.

[4] Straker 1931, pp. 276–7; Schubert, 1957, p. 370.

[5] K.A.O., U1475 B4/1 (Kent Archives Office, Maidstone). Reprinted in D. W. Crossley (ed.) *The Sidney Ironworks Accounts*, Camden 4th Series. Vol. 15 (1975), 207.

[6] *Valor Ecclesiasticus*, Record Commission, 1 (1810), 79.

[7] P.R.O., SC6/1762–8.

[8] *Letters and Papers* (L. & P.), Henry VIII, 1543 pt. 1 (1901), p. 545.

[9] Ibid., 1540 (1896), p. 472.

purchased Chingley manor and Chingley Wood from the Crown,[1] and in 1546 resold to Stephen Darell of Horsmonden, keeping only some distant lands at Staplehurst.[2]

The Darells were a prominent family, Thomas Darell, Stephen's brother, being sheriff of Surrey and Sussex in 1541,[3] and they had occupied Scotney Castle from the fifteenth century.[4] Their lands could usefully be extended eastwards and southwards from Scotney Park by this purchase, adding further timber, iron ore and water rights. Thomas Darell of Scotney was fully aware by the end of the 1540s of the potential of ironmaking; in 1548-9 he was a member of a Commission which enquired into Iron Mills in the Rape of Hastings, and he appended a particular report on a forge set up in the 1540s between Lamberhurst and Wadhurst, commenting on the local disquiet caused by its timber consumption.[5] Both Stephen and Thomas Darell died in 1558, but neither in Stephen's Inquisition Post Mortem nor in Thomas's will[6] is there any mention of a furnace, nor in the quitclaim of Chingley manor made by Stephen to his nephew, Thomas jr, in 1558.[7] This is as close to 1565 as we can get; all, it must be stressed, with negative evidence. However, the period from 1558 (when the younger Thomas took charge of the estate) to 1565 does seem the best estimate for a construction date. Certainly the next dated lease of the furnace began in 1579,[8] so if there had been a previous tenant, on a 21-year lease, this would reinforce a date close to 1558 for original construction.

The information becomes very much firmer in the 1570s. The furnace was entered in the returns to the 1574 enquiry into Weald Ironworks as belonging to Thomas Darell and operated by Thomas Dyke of Horsmonden.[9] In this return the Forge was still not mentioned. Dyke is a relatively well-known figure, operating Derondale Forge, near Pembury, in 1574, and taking on Serenden furnace, Horsmonden, another site owned by Thomas Darell, in 1579.[10] The Darells, also, were active. Apart from Thomas's interests, his brother Christopher set up Ewood furnace in Surrey in 1553, a site which, through chequered ownerships and finances, remained at least partially in the family until 1588 or later.[11]

The furnace seems still to have been workable in 1579, for in that year a syndicate comprising Thomas Darell, Henry his son, Edmund Pelham and Thomas Dyke let Chingley Furnace, and other lands including part of Scotney Park, to Dyke alone for 41 years.[12] At this time the Darells appear to have been selling and letting lands, and in 1581 a good deal of Chingley Manor, without the furnace or, probably, Chingley Wood,

---

[1] Ibid., 1544 pt. 2 (1905), p. 414.
[2] Ibid., 1546 (1910), p. 168.
[3] P.R.O., *Lists and Indexes*, IX, Lists of Sheriffs (1963), 137.
[4] See p. 2, note 1.
[5] Historical Manuscripts Commission: *Manuscripts of the Marquis of Salisbury*, XIII (1914), 21-4. Reprinted in R. H. Tawney and E. Power, *Tudor Economic Documents* (London, 1924), I, 231-8.
[6] P.R.O., C142/123/98; K.A.O., U409/Z3 (transcript).
[7] E.S.R.O., Danny MS 1442 (East Sussex Record Office, Lewes).
[8] E.S.R.O., Dyke-Hutton MS 607.
[9] Several versions of the 1574 list have survived, in P.R.O. SP/12/95, 96 and 117, and in B. M. Stowe MS 570, p. 103. One, from SP/12/117 is published by D. and G. Mathew, 'Iron Furnaces in South-east England...'. *English Historical Review*, XLVIII (1933), 91 et seq.
[10] E.S.R.O. Dyke-Hutton MS 606.
[11] Straker 1931, pp. 451-6.
[12] E.S.R.O. Dyke-Hutton MS 607.

was sold to Edmund Pelham.[1] There is the presumption in the deed that Chingley furnace was still in operation, for wayleaves and pond rights are defined with some care, these encroaching on the ground bought by Pelham. By 1588, the date of a further survey of ironworks, the furnace was recorded as 'fallen downe and utterlie decayed'.[2] The last firm reference is in 1597, when Dyke transferred his 41-year lease of the wood dating from 1579 to Richard Ballard and his sons. There is no comment about the state or any rebuilding of the furnace, but considerable detail and emphasis on the woodlands.[3]

Turning to the forge, this was clearly not in operation in 1574, but at the time of the second enquiry, in 1588–90, Richard Ballard was the tenant 'to make owt bars of Iron'.[4] About 1595 more of Chingley manor was sold to Edmund Pelham and James Thetcher, of whom the first was clearly on the lookout for land in the area, the 'forge or yron workes called Chingley forge' being included.[5] In 1628–9 pig iron was brought to the forge from Snape furnace,[6] and in 1637 William Darell, by this time part-owner of Scotney and Chingley, leased the estate including iron forges and ironworks to Henry Darell of Clerkenwell and two others for 15 years, and Chingley Wood for 20 years.[7]

What happened during the Civil War is not clear. There was an involved dispute in 1650–4 over the sequestration of the Darell lands, but in none of the papers is a working forge mentioned, merely 'one other farm there (in Goudhurst) called the forge land', in the tenure of William Baldock in 1649.[8] The forge is omitted from the 1653 and 1664 sections of the list of ironworks of 1664.[9]

It is not known when the site was refurbished. It appears in Fuller's list of 1717,[10] and on Budgen's map of 1724.[11] The Scotney papers include the reference quoted by

[1] E.S.R.O. Danny MSS 1445–6. There is a good deal of confusion about this. Straker claims (p. 277) that Darell sold the manor in 1589 to Sir Edward Culpepper, who, in turn, sold to Edward Pelham and James Fletcher (properly *Thetcher*) 'about 1626'. He cites G. W. Loder, *Wakehurst* (London, 1907), p. 52 as his source, but in fact in his book Loder says nothing about Culpepper's purchase from Darell, and puts the sale to Thetcher and Pelham at 1595. The answer probably lies in the section of the Danny (Wakehurst) MSS that never reached E.S.R.O. and whose fate is unknown. There seems no doubt that Chingley manor was sold by the Darells piecemeal, for the Furnace and Forge lands are not within the carefully described bounds in the 1581 document. It could well be that Culpepper, and in turn Pelham and Thetcher, took on the remaining ground around 1595 (see note 5 below). Straker's reference to a sale in 1626 can probably be discounted, although clearly there were later transfers, as the Darells were back in possession in 1637 (see n. 7 below); they, the Catsfield Pelhams, and the Thetchers, were all members of the recusant group in the district.
[2] Staffs.R.O. Sutherland MS D593/S/4/28/3: 'Henry Darell, gent, hath in Chingley within the parish of Growthurst only a fordge or hamro now in the occupacon of Rycherd Ballard but the furnace that was thear is fallen downe and utterlie decayed'. For discussion of the Sutherland documents see C. S. Cattell, 'An Evaluation of the Loseley List . . .' *Archaeologia Cantiana*, 86 (1971), 85–92.
[3] E.S.R.O. Dyke-Hutton MS 607. There is no evidence that Ballard rebuilt the furnace, to operate it with the forge.
[4] Staffordshire Record Office, D593/S/4/28/11.
[5] G. W. Loder, *Wakehurst* (London, 1907), p. 52 (but see note 1 above).
[6] E.S.R.O., Quarter Sessions Records: Lewes 15 January 1629.
[7] P.R.O. SP23/67/811.
[8] SP23/67/787. The records of the Committee for Compounding dealing with this case are scattered, due to the involvement of the two County Committees, for Sussex and Kent. SP23/67 and 113 contain the bulk of the useful material. An undated deed in K.A.O. Scotney MSS (U409/T52) also refers to William Baldock of Wadhurst as tenant of the Forge land. It is highly likely that Old Forge Farm (p. 41) was the house for this tenement.
[9] J. L. Parsons, in 'The Sussex Ironworks', *Sussex Archaeological Collections*, 32 (1882), 19–32 prints the list.
[10] E. W. Hulme, 'Statistical History of the Iron Trade of England and Wales', *Transactions of the Newcomen Society*, 9 (1928–9), 12–35. Hulme used the pamphlet *The Interest of Great Britain in Supplying herself with Iron* of 1717, and a later anonymous list, dated 1736 by Hulme, which states 'of the last four (including Chingley) no Account, but their names in an old list' (1717).
[11] West Sussex R.O., PM 47.

Straker to John Legas as tenant of the forge in 1726.[1] Legas operated Gloucester Furnace, a mile west of Lamberhurst,[2] and although production at Chingley, according to Fuller, was only 46 tons a year it could well have been valuable to Legas for forging capacity if only to meet peaks in his production of pig iron. However, the Scotney collection does not provide a date of closure; a list of Chingley properties of 1735 does not include it, but as one in comparable format for 1726 omitted it, no conclusions can be drawn. However, the forge has no production returned in the list of 1736 printed by Hulme. An abstract of title dating from 1768 refers to the forge, but with no indication that it was capable of working.[3]

Perhaps most interesting of the late records is the map of Scotney estate of 1828,[4] based on a survey by Clout of 1759. This shows the Forge Pond in water, covering 6 acres, the Forge Field, to the south-east of the site, the Pit Field further south, and Pond Field to the south-west of the tail of the pond. The representation of the pond probably dates from the original survey,[5] and, as no forge buildings are shown, may suggest that they were demolished by 1759.

[1] K.A.O. U409/T2.
[2] K.A.O. U120/C52/1.
[3] Hulme, ibid., K.A.O. U409/T2.
[4] U409/P48 – U769/Z1–2. By this time the estate had been bought by Edward Hussey.
[5] The First Edition 1-inch Ordnance Survey (1813) shows no pond.

III The Excavation

In order to clarify the subsequent sections, the differences between medieval and later iron-smelting methods should be stressed. In the bloomery comparatively small quantities of low-carbon malleable iron were produced in a bloomhearth, only requiring reheating in a stringhearth and hammering under a tilt-hammer to extract the remaining slag and to shape into bar iron. However, blast furnaces, introduced into the Weald at the end of the fifteenth century, produced a brittle high-carbon cast iron, requiring refining into a malleable bloom in the finery hearth, and then hammering into bar, with intermittent reheating in a chafery hearth. For further details reference should be made to Schubert and Tylecote.

THE FORGE

The site was easily found from the comments of earlier field-workers. Straker had noted scatters of cinder around the head of what he assumed to be a 'hammerdyke' and the Archaeology Division of the Ordnance Survey had identified the head of this ditch at (N.G.R.) TQ 68253348.[1] This was indeed the tailrace, running north from the

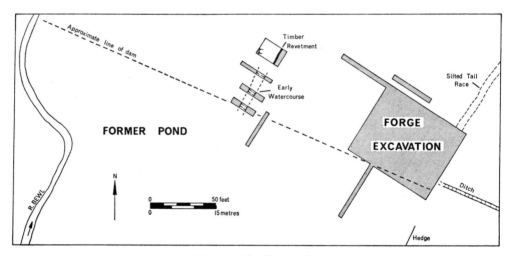

Fig. 2. The Forge site

wheel-pits of Period III (p. 23 below) to join the Bewl at 68353372 (Fig. 1:3). It started from a patch of drier ground on which mole-hills and tractor-ruts showed deposits of forge-cinder and charcoal. Close inspection before the growth of summer grass showed a slight ridge across the field (Fig. 2) passing to the south of this area of cinders, and

[1] From reference card held in the Ordnance Survey Archaeology Division index, Southampton.

corresponding with the dam shown on Clout's survey of 1759.[1] The hillslope to the south-east had a distinct scarp, indicating where the edge of the pond once lay.

An initial trial cutting confirmed the whereabouts of the site, locating the outflow from the stone-lined race of Period III.

The major periods defined during the excavation will be described in order of deposit.

PERIOD I (Figs. 3–10; Pls. I–VA; APPENDIX)

The Race

The major feature was a wheel-race built of oak timbers and in an excellent state of preservation, with associated material suggesting use in about 1300. This was the earliest of three wheel-pits, shown schematically in Fig. 3.

A trench approximately 7 ft wide had been dug in the natural gravel and alluvium to accommodate the base-frame for the race. A two-bay frame had been laid, each bay being 9 ft long and 3 ft wide, between inside faces of the timbers; it comprised three cross-sleepers linked by two pairs of longitudinal members, of uneven section generally 9–10 in. wide and 5–7 in. deep. The detailed dimensions of the timbers and joints in this structure are given in the Appendix, p. 37. Housed tenons had been used (Pl. IV), cut to approximately the width of the longitudinal beams except in the north-west joint of the north bay and the north-east joint of the south bay (Fig. 4). The one exception was the north-west joint of the south bay (Pl. IIIB), a dovetail, suggesting that this western long member had been dropped in at a late stage. While there was no sign of an abandoned mortice in the centre sleeper to suggest that the different method indicated later work, the adjacent upright (Fig. 4) was small enough in section to permit the dovetail to be dropped in.

The next stage had been to place a vertical member at the corner of each bay, and three along each cross-sleeper, one to the west and two to the east of the race in each case. These all had full-width tenons, all 4 in. long and slightly chamfered. The uprights varied in section, as is shown in Fig. 4. All were of oak and were 2 ft 1 in. long excluding their top and bottom tenons.[2] Intermediate posts, along the sides of the bays, were of lighter section, typically $9 \times 6\frac{1}{2}$ in. All were of oak. Each was set in a mortice in the base frame, the tenons being of uniform length at $3\frac{1}{2}$ in. and slightly chamfered. All these smaller uprights (Pl. IIIA) were water-worn, but the least abraded suggested that the tenons were about $\frac{1}{2}$ in. less in width than the main posts. Edge-set longitudinal oak boards had been put two-high behind the intermediate uprights along the race; clearly along the east side, and possibly along the west, these had been renewed during the life of the site, water-wheel sideboards had been used in the northern bay (east side) (Fig. 7b; Pl. I). Their dimensions are discussed on p. 42.

Much of the filling around the lower part of the structure contained thirteenth-century pottery. The earliest deposits were 9F and 9G, the original fillings around the base frame and behind the sideboards, and also partly filling the end of the main trench where it had been dug needlessly far to the south. On the west side this was covered by 9K,

---

[1] K.A.O. U409/P48. Map of Scotney Estate, 1828, based on a survey by Clout, 1759 (see p. 13 below).
[2] Samples taken for dendrochronological examination proved unsuitable for this purpose; growth of the wood had been so rapid that only 65–70 rings could be measured.

B

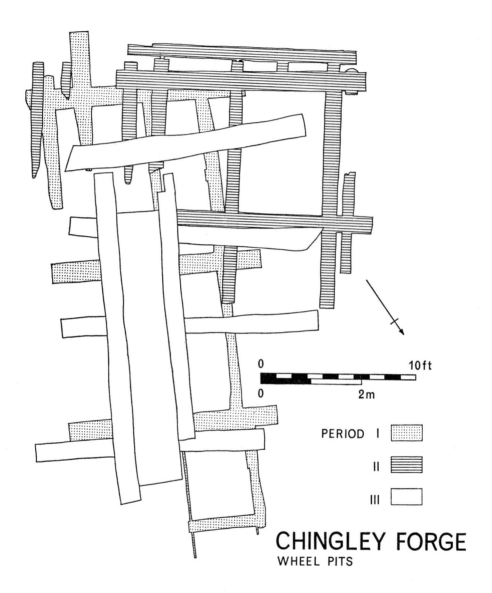

Fig. 3.   The Forge: diagram of wheel-pits, Periods I–III

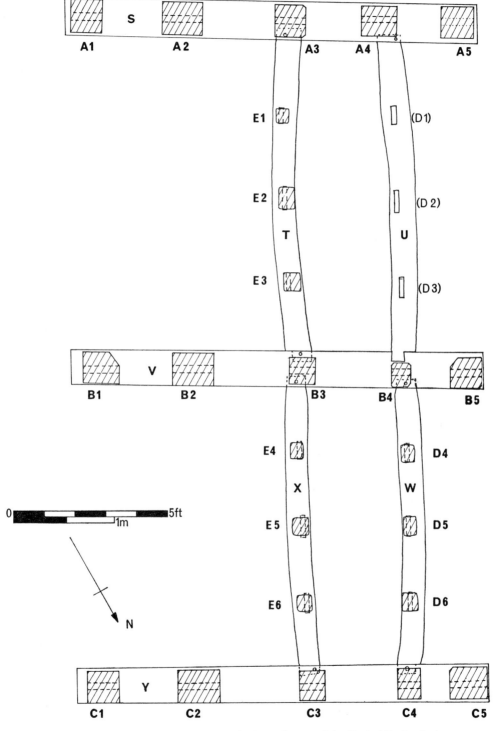

Fig. 4.   The Forge: The base-frame of the Period I wheel-pit.
Numbering of timbers corresponds with Appendix

which may have been inserted during the replacement of sideboards. On the east side it was clear that 9H (south bay) and 9J (north bay) had been deposited thus, their sandy, stony composition distinguishing them from the original filling below, into which those replacing the boards had cut. 9G, 9H, and 9J contained grey wares typical of those seen in the excavation of Kentish sites dating from the second half of the thirteenth century (discussed below, p. 48).

The tops of each of the three rows of major verticals running across the site had also been shaped as tenons, and on these had stood three substantial oak cross-beams, surviving fragments being 15 in. wide and 12–12½ in. thick. These had been set with their top surfaces close to the level of the adjacent undisturbed natural ground, and their eastern ends were in trenches cut to as much as 16 in. deep to achieve this. Parts of these cross-beams (Fig. 6) had survived in position, the missing lengths having been removed during the construction of Period II.

The uppermost elements in the structure (Fig. 7c) were beams (Pl. IIA) running north-south, parallel with the race. Fragments of two survived at the south-east corner of the frame, and these had been secured to the southern upper cross-member by lapped dovetail joints giving a positive location, suggesting that they were designed to withstand a good deal of stress. The eastern member was 7 ft 6 in. overall from the eastern inner edge of the race. The total number and character of these uppermost timbers must remain in doubt. There were faint traces of a dovetail seating on the southern upper cross-member in line with the eastern side of the race; further, the intermediate uprights along this side of the race had tenons to fit a further long top timber. However, the centre and southern upper cross-members showed no evidence of joints, and the only feasible suggestion is that this long timber was half-jointed, with no corresponding cut-out in the cross-members. Much the same applies to the timber along the western side of the race, but here there were no traces of a dovetail, for the cross-member had been cut away to accommodate Period II timbers, and had rotted. There was no evidence for a north–south top timber west of the race, and none has been conjectured in Fig. 7c.

The careful and uniform workmanship of the builders needs emphasis. Variations in section between uprights were uncommon, and many of the mortice and tenon joints were virtually interchangeable. This applied in particular to the intermediate posts. All the vertical members' tenons were measured, but time and difficult site conditions prevented more than approximate measurements being taken of the tenons of the base frame. The information recovered is summarized in the Appendix, p. 37.

In the north bay was found a fragment of a water-wheel (Figs. 5a, 6, 9a) consisting of one sideboard and three bucket boards, all of oak. It had been approximately 8 ft 3 in. in diameter, and 1 ft 1 in. wide between sideboards. It could not be proved that it lay in its original position, but if it did, its configuration would necessarily make it part of an overshot rather than a pitch-back or breast-wheel. However, its distance from the dam raises problems over why there should have been another bay to the south, over which a penstock or launder would have to have been built. The best possible answers might be the placing of two wheels in tandem, or that the fragment excavated had operated in the southern bay. Wheel-fragments found in layers 8H/8J are discussed on p. 42.

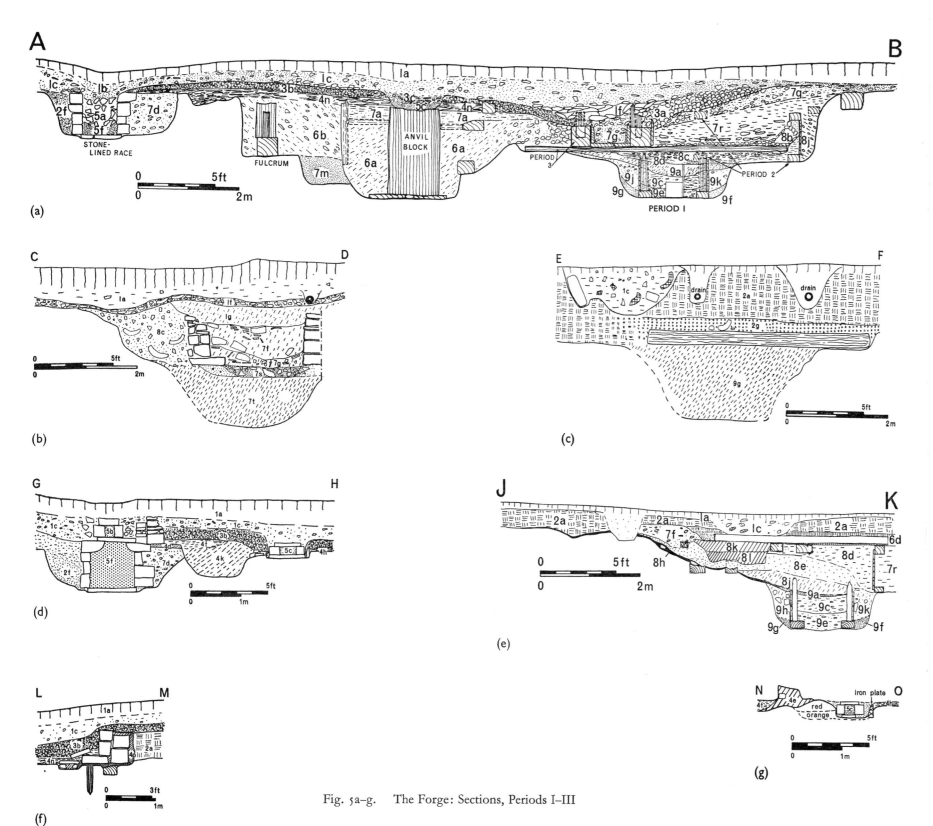

Fig. 5a–g. The Forge: Sections, Periods I–III

5a   A–B Section across the Forge, Periods I–III.
5b   C–D Section across tailraces, Periods I–III.
       The build-up of silt (7t) fills the tailraces I and II. The western edge of the early race was unstable and the section here is approximate. The eastern face of the stonework of race III was not removed due to unstable ground conditions.
5c   E–F Section along face of the dam showing trench for Period III penstock. The horizontal timber relates to Period II. See plan: Fig 11.
5d   G–H Section across Period IIIA race, showing entrenched race, with later stone field drain above, cinder pit in finery building and (right: 5c) field drain cutting through west end of finery.
5e   J–K Section across wheel-pit I and overlying features of II and IIIB.
5f   L–M Section indicating timber beam and stake below stone front to dam.
5g   N–O Part-section indicating zones of heating in the natural clay beneath the finery hearth.

LAYERS

1a   Topsoil.
1b   Upper silts over IIIA race.
1c   Rubble and topsoil.
1f   Silt over IIIB wheel-pit.
1g   Silt.
2a   Clay: dam, Period III and perhaps II.
2f   Clay filling of IIIA race foundation trench (east side).
2g   Clay: dam, Period II.
3a   Heavy black cinder overlying working levels east of IIIB wheel-pit.
3b   Black cinder and tile overlying forge floor working levels.
3c   Cinder, charcoal and tile fragments at south-west end of stone field drain.
4d   Cinder beneath finery east wall.
4e   Purple hearth material.
4f   Cinder: floor debris in finery building.
4h   Hard cinder: working debris: Period III.
4k   Cinder: filling of pit in finery.
4n   Hard cinder: working debris of Period III.
4p   Dark soil: fill of dam-head wall trench, overlying timber probably of Period II.
5a   Silt and rubble: IIIA race.
5b   Silt: east field drain.
5c   Silt: west field drain.
5f   Silt: IIIA race.
6a   Clay and stones: filling of IIIB anvil pit.
6b   Clay and stones: filling of IIIA hammer fulcrum pit.
6d   Pink clay, packing around IIIB southern timber.
7a   Cinder and wood chips: upper filling.
7d   Clay and stones: filling of IIIA race foundation (west side).
7f   Dark clay and charcoal, around IIIB hammer frame, extending towards dam.
7g   Silt: IIIB race. Tile fragments.
7m   Sandy: fill of ?IIIA anvil pit.
7q   Cinder and grey soil; working floor west of IIIB race, around small anvil.
7r   Dark grey clay with hearth bottoms of slag; build-up for IIIB over II.
7s   First silt of III. Tile fragments.
7t   Clay silty fill with wood debris, continuing from 9a, 9b (Section A–B).
8b   Clay and rusty cinder: dump within II wheel-pit, around III sleepers.
8c   Silt and cinder: early dump within II wheel-pit. Tile fragments.
8d   Blue-grey clay; first dump in II wheel-pit, and behind side-boards on the east. Probably laid during construction or use of II. Some tile fragments.
8h   Soil, charcoal, tiles, wood chips: Period I working level.
8j   Brown clay around wheel-pit II side-boards. Perhaps laid in Period II, but with residual material from I.
8k   Possible hammer scale, packed round II timbers.
8l   Similar to 8k, but harder.
9a   Black mossy silt sealing lower silts in wheel-pit I.
9c   Blue stiff clay with wood chips in wheel-pit I, built up in and around wheel fragment. Tile fragments.
9e   Gritty silt with water-worn stones. Tile fragments.
9f   Sandy: Period I, west side, early filling.
9g   Sandy with stones: I, east side, early filling.
9h   Stones and sand: I, east side, filling of repair trench (south bay). Tile fragments.
9k   Stones and sand: I, west side, filling of repair trench.

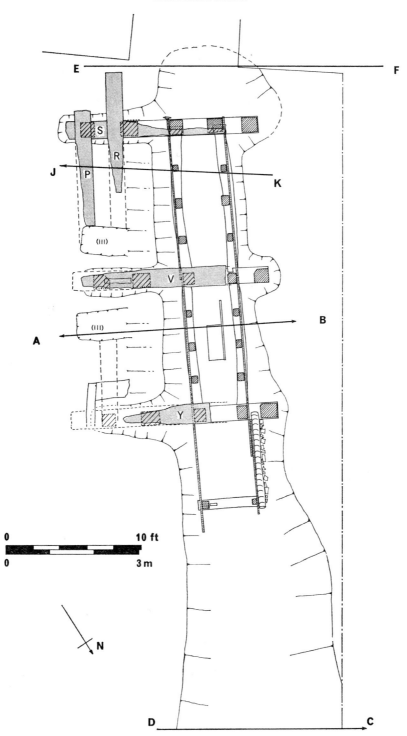

Fig. 6.   The Forge: Period I, plan of the timber structure (surviving upper members shaded).
For sections see Fig. 5. Disturbance from Period IIIв marked: (III).
Numbering of timbers corresponds with Appendix

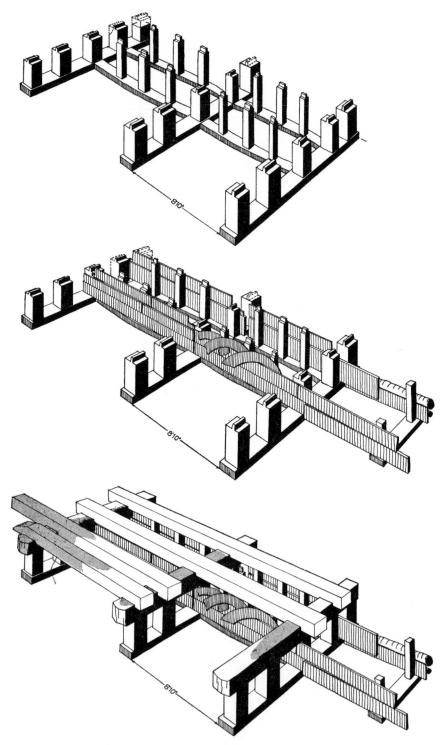

Fig. 7A–C The Forge: Period I — Perspective reconstructions

(A) Base-frame and verticals
(B) With side-boards
(C) With upper horizontal members (surviving timber shaded)

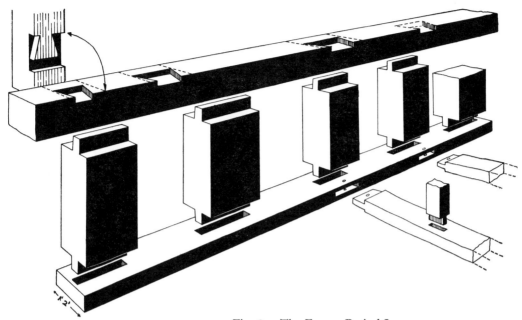

Fig. 8. The Forge: Period I.
Perspective detail of southern end of wheel-pit structure

Northwards from the main structure the tailrace first ran between roughly-set sides almost 8 ft long, mounted against a pair of uprights set in a further transverse sleeper. The western sideboards rested against a log wedged against the natural. Further north, the tailrace was no more than a wide ill-defined hollow (Fig. 5b) in which had accumulated quantities of silt and vegetation (layer 7T), with some thirteenth-century pottery.

To the west of the wheel-race the ground surface had been removed during later use of the site, but to the east the sloping surface of sand, weathered sandstone and alluvium was covered with a thin layer of charcoal, with small quantities of cinder and slag (Fig. 5e). This layer (8H) contained quantities of pottery, largely unglazed grey wares, with some green-glazed sherds. Bones and shell indicating workers' diet are referred to on p. 43. Such material also appeared in residual deposits over the infilling (9A) of the race. Tiles in 9C and 9E suggested that the structure had been roofed.

To this dating evidence should be added pottery from deposits in the wheel-race itself. In the bottom layer 9E were quantities of grey wares, and in 9C, above, was similar material, and a sherd of Rye ware with raspberry-stamp decoration. In 9E there were, in addition, sheet brass and lead scrap, a fragment of brass crucible, nails, and a knife. In the silts above 9C (9A and 9B) there were no datable objects.

The dam and water supply

It was not satisfactorily established how water reached the site in this period. The section through the later dam (Fig. 10) shows an early bank of blue-grey clay which was

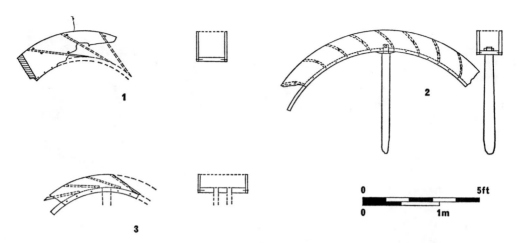

Fig. 9A.   The Forge and Furnace. Fragments of overshot water-wheels

1. Forge: Period I   2. Furnace   3. Forge: Period IIIB, chafery

broadened northwards in the construction of Period II. It is not certain whether this was the original dam, or merely a first dump for the sixteenth-century construction. The lack of a turf line on the north slope of the first clay suggests the latter. What may be significant is that no vestige of an early dam was found in the north–south cutting to the west (Fig. 2). This, and others, made by machine, showed a wide depression in what would be the centre of the valley, and thus perhaps the original channel of the Bewl. It was aligned north to south with logs roughly revetting the eastern edge, perhaps to prevent erosion towards the forge. This adds weight to the suggestion that there was either a small pond, on the eastern side of the stream, or none at all, with water being carried in a leat from further upstream.

The function of the site

There are three obvious uses for a water-mill foundation of this period: the milling of grain, the fulling of cloth, or the operation of bellows and hammers for iron smelting. While the first two cannot be totally ruled out,[1] the material found on the site emphasizes the last possibility, although not without certain problems. The charcoal dust scattered to the east of the race and the tap-slag in and around it suggest smelting, and the presence of scrap and specialized metal objects such as brass buckles indicates that the occupiers were familiar with a range of metal crafts.

However, one puzzling feature was the small quantity of tap-slag, relative to other sites of the bloomery period. This may suggest that smelting had been done elsewhere, that the blooms of iron had been carted to the site for hammering, and the slag had come fortuitously, dropped perhaps from carts at times used for slag removal from a smelting

---

[1] There was certainly a mill on Chingley manor in the 1340s (P.R.O. SC6/889/1–6), but whether it was a wind- or water-mill is not stated, and nor is its position, which could have been anywhere on the Bewl from above Dunsters Mill (TQ 689323) to Bewl Bridge (686347), or on the tributary joining the Bewl near Overys Farm (693322) which flows through *Mill Wood*, which may or may not relate to Dunsters.

site, or brought for some constructional or levelling purpose at the forge. Clearly this is not conclusive, as tap-slag could have been cleared away during operations, to some dumping point outside the excavated area. However, at this period well-developed yet unpowered bloomeries were operating in the higher woodlands of the Weald. An excellent example is the site at Minepit Wood, Withyham, recently excavated,[1] and the blooms made at such a site, where no forge was found, could have been removed for hammering at a valley-bottom forge comparable with Chingley, possessing a tilt hammer and a string hearth for reheating.

If this hypothesis is to be pursued, indications of hammer and anvil must be sought. It was common practice in the sixteenth and seventeenth centuries to place an anvil on a timber block, often a length of tree-trunk, set vertically in a pit, on a timber foundation. There was no such pit within either bay of the eastward extension of the timber foundation, as would probably have been required had a hammer-beam operated at right-angles to the wheel and cam spindle. If the beam were parallel with the spindle, the pit could have been placed further to the east, depending on the length of the beam. There was no trace of such a pit-foundation to correspond with a water-wheel in the south bay of the race; however, in line with the north bay, in which the wheel-fragment was in fact found, there had subsequently been excavated the anvil pit for the seventeenth-century forge, which could have obliterated a predecessor. Here there was a trace of a shallower excavation (Fig. 5a) on the western edge of the late pit, possibly the remnant of an early one.

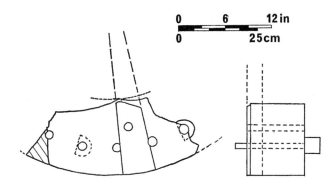

Fig. 9B.   Fragment of gear-wheel. Period I

A fragment of a gearwheel found on the early working deposit indicates that other equipment was operated. As will be seen from Fig. 9b it comprised an oak rim 48 in. in diameter, made up of at least 5 sectors, spoked to a centre. Part of one of these sectors had survived together with numerous worn oak peg-teeth of the kind familiar from Agricola.[2] The close pitch of the teeth made it rather unlikely that the gear operated a hammer helve directly, unless a very rapidly-working plating hammer had been used on

[1] J. H. Money, 'Medieval Iron-workings in Minepit Wood, Rotherfield, Sussex', Medieval Archaeology, 15 (1971), 86–111.
[2] G. Agricola, De Re Metallica (Basle, 1556, ed. H. and L. Hoover, New York, 1950), p. 372.

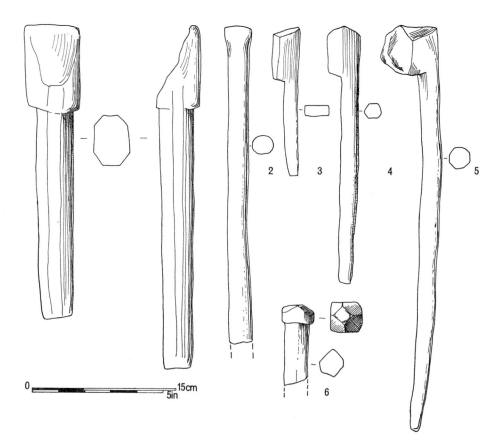

Fig. 9c.   Gear pegs. Period I

small blooms. It is more likely that it was used for some form of right-angle drive, via a further camshaft, either to the hammer, or, more likely, off the end of the hammer shaft to a bellows camshaft. It certainly seems that the rate of wear and discard was high, for the teeth found scattered along the edge of the race were well worn down. Indeed the designer of the wheel had clearly envisaged the need for easy replacement of the teeth.

The abandonment of Period I

The end of operations cannot have been far beyond the middle of the fourteenth century, for amongst the pottery there was an absence of the wares which appear in other Kentish sites at this time. After abandonment there appears to have been a considerable accumulation of silt in the wheel-pit, material whose gradations and accumulations of vegetable matter did not suggest deliberate dumping for foundations for later structures. It seems that there was no further activity until late in the sixteenth century.

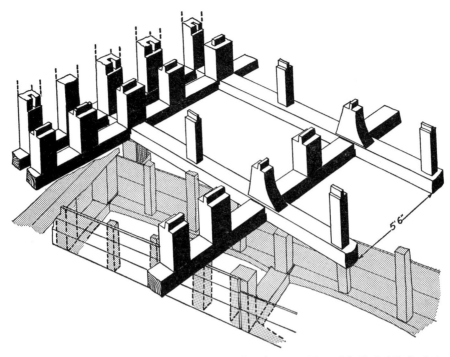

(A)   The base frame and verticals, indicating the relative position of the Period I wheel-pit

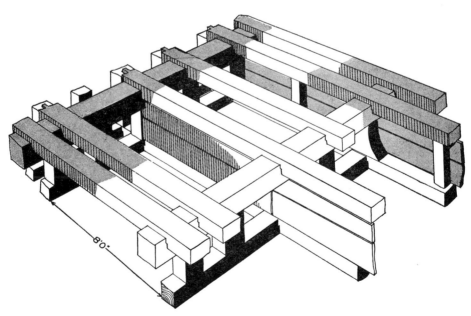

(B)   The probable form of the complete structure, with the surviving upper horizontals shaded

Fig. 12.   A and B.   The Forge: perspective reconstructions of
the wheel-pit of Period II

end of the sixteenth century and later, rather than the Dissolution period. Food bones were absent and shells were sparse. As will be seen below (p. 23), the life of this second structure may have extended into the seventeenth century until or even beyond the building of the stone race of Period IIIA.

The new structure was wider than the old; three substantial oak cross-sleepers were laid, each 10½ in. wide by 8 in. deep (see Appendix). Half-jointed on to these sleepers were two longitudinal members, 9½ in. wide by 6¼ in. deep. This base had been laid making little use of the timbers of the early race, which appeared to have been silted and forgotten after a lapse of over 200 years. When an early timber was encountered it was chopped through, though some may have been removed altogether. A clear example is shown in Fig. 12a, where the early southern upper cross-member received a tapering cut to accommodate the end of the new base frame. Two early uprights were cut down to act as supports (Pl. IIB).

The alignment of this base differed by 10 degrees from the old one, and the new tailrace took an easterly course, later partially filled to build the chafery wheel-pit late in the seventeenth century. The structure lay at a higher level than that of Period I, the base being only 4–6 in. below the tops of the tenons of the intermediate verticals of the early race. Even though laid at this level, excavation westwards had been needed to accommodate the extra width.

Into the base were set tenoned uprights, 1 ft 8 in. high, excluding tenons (Figs. 12a, 13a), which supported an upper horizontal frame. The main uprights were generally uniform in section, typically 12½ in. by 8½ in. (Appendix). However, the intermediate posts along the side of the wheel-pit and the massive member surviving half-way along the west side were smaller and larger respectively (Fig. 13b). A similar large member appears to have been set on the east side of the frame, indicated by the size of the appropriate mortice (Fig. 11). The southernmost line of verticals (Pl. VI) had clearly been longer, to support a penstock. The uprights had been encased in edge-set planks (Figs. 11, 12b, and Pl. VI), confirming the extent of the wheel-pit; there was no clear explanation for the continuation of the planks eastwards from the back of the wheel-pit. It will be seen from Figs. 13a and 13b that where a vertical was set above a half-joint in the base-frame the lower base member was morticed, enabling the long tenon of the upright to give added rigidity to the half-joint.

The upper horizontals had been largely destroyed during Period III, but fragments and joints provided some evidence of their form. Two substantial beams had been set east-to-west across the tenons of the lines of uprights. On to these had been half-jointed six north–south beams, the surviving fragments of which are shown shaded in Fig. 12b. Only the middle four had been tenoned to the southernmost verticals. There must remain a measure of uncertainty over the easterly four of the top members, but Fig. 12b provides a reconstruction based on the surviving mortice slots in the lower frame. In addition to these six beams, a further two lay to the east, resting on made-up ground (Fig. 11).

The function of this frame is of great interest. It will be seen from Fig. 12b that within the edge-set plank lining there was a double chamber; this is interpreted as a double wheel-pit, for two water wheels mounted on a common spindle, the spindle-bearings, either two or three, being set on the upper long members. The use of a pair

PERIOD II (Figs. 3, 5, 10–13; Pls. IIB, V–VI, IX; APPENDIX)

In the late sixteenth century a new wheel-pit was built, partly over the earlier structure. Its relation to Period I can be seen from Figs. 3 and 12a. The most convincing estimate for its date of construction must be the period between 1574 and 1588, for Chingley Forge was included in the list of Wealden Ironworks compiled in the latter year, but not in that of 1574. There were very few stratified finds relating to this period; a spade (Fig. 33) sealed beneath the western longitudinal base-beam was of a pattern typical of the sixteenth century, although having a long life. The pottery was sparse, but fits the

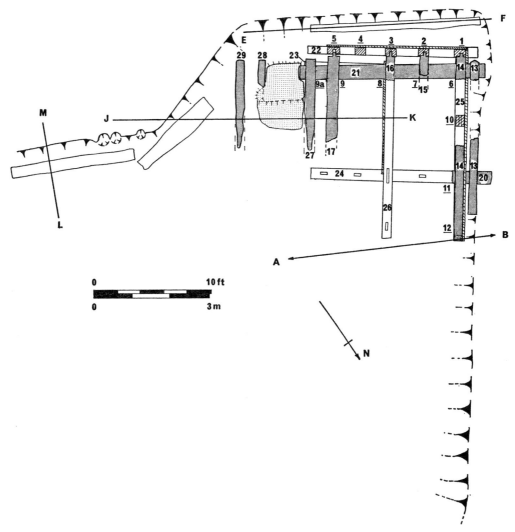

Fig. 11. The Forge: plan of Period II structure, with upper members shaded. The numbers refer to Appendix and those underlined denote vertical timbers, mostly hidden in plan. For the marked sections, refer to Fig. 5

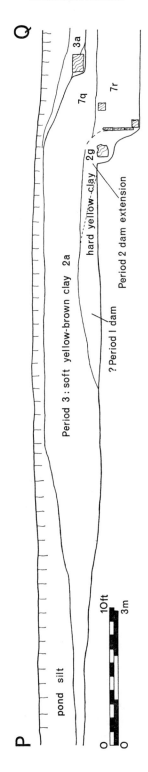

Fig. 10. The Forge. Section through Dam (see plan, Fig. 14)

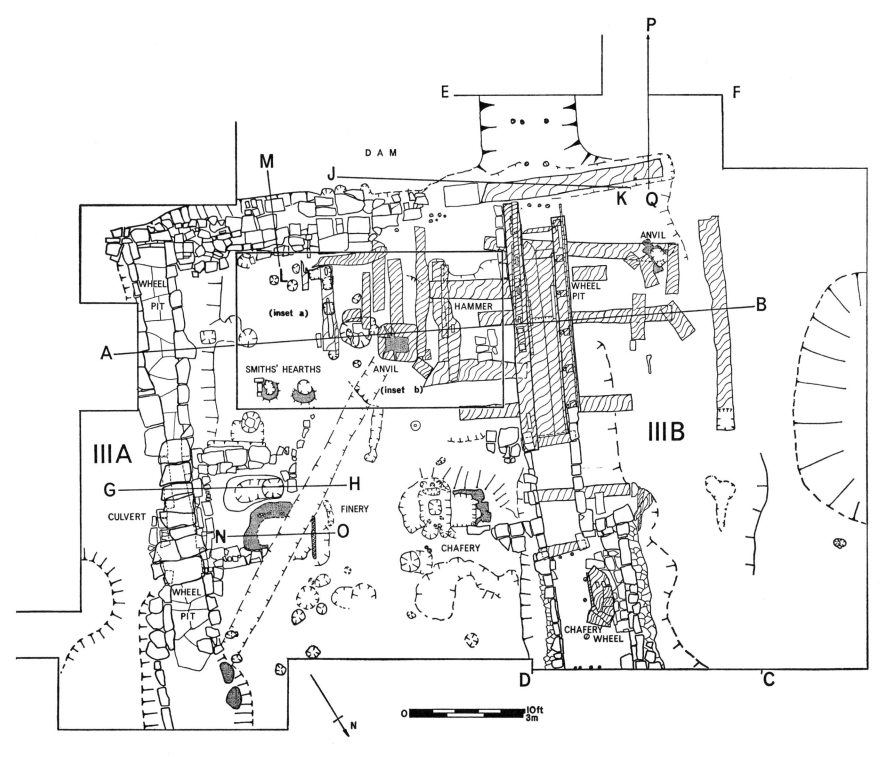

Fig. 14.   The Forge. Plan of Period III. For the marked sections, refer to Fig. 5. For insets (a and b) refer to Fig 15.

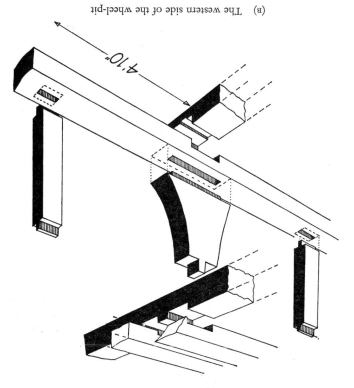

(b) The western side of the wheel-pit

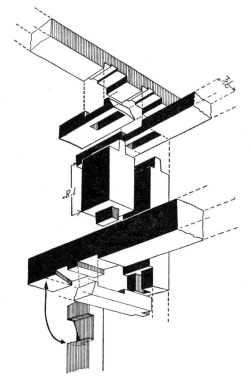

(a) The south-west corner

Fig. 13. A and B. The Forge: perspective details of the Period II timberwork

of wheels had attractions at this period. It allowed a relatively high torque to be developed, when to do this with one wheel meant either great width or large diameter, both of which posed problems of rigid construction and thus of reliability. Sixteenth-century water wheels were often flimsily built, as is clear from contemporary paintings, and ironworks accounts show how frequently repairs were needed.[1]

The use to which the wheels were put raises similar problems to those of Period I. A hammer seems, again, the most likely, this time with rather more documentary support, and, again, it must be suggested that the anvil-foundation had been altered for the hammer of Period IIIB. It would be entirely feasible for the four eastern timbers to have supported a fulcrum for a hammer whose tail-helve would be operated by cams on the wheel-shaft, and whose anvil centre need be no more than 7 ft west of that found in situ for Period IIIB. The only argument against this arises from the hard deposit, perhaps of hammer scale among the eastern timbers (Fig. 11). It is just possible that a nose-helve hammer, pivoted to the north and operated by a wheel-spindle, worked on to a surface-mounted anvil close to this deposit. However, this seems far from likely as the strength and power capacity of the wheel emplacement suggests the need for a pit-set anvil. Further, the possible scale was not evenly deposited, and may have been brought as build-up for the back of the later breast-wheel shroud.

The dam for this wheel-pit was a substantial deposit of yellow clay, which overlay the thirteenth-century working debris and the southern end of the early race. The clay stretched across the field, being visible in a machine-cut trench and in the banks of the Bewl. At the forge, it was revetted with horizontal timber kerbs. One (Figs. 5c and 11) was parallel with, and 2 ft south of the line of the back of the wheel-pit, and stains and fragments of further wood survived to the east, where the dam was wider. Although the stratification was broken by a field-drain trench, the association of these timbers with the clay was relatively certain (Fig. 5f). How large a pond this had been is uncertain due to the difficulty of assessing the height of the dam. Levelling had been thorough in the nineteenth century and, further, there was no way to tell whether the prominent scarping of the eastern edge of the pond area belonged to this or a later period.

This evidence leaves unanswered the layout of the rest of the site. A finery forge of the late sixteenth century comprised not only a hammer but finery and chafery hearths to convert pig-iron into bar. These also required water power, to operate their bellows. There were no such features to relate to the second race, and it is to the next stage of development that we must look for guidance. While the stone-lined race on the east of the site (IIIA) appears, in the form in which it was excavated, to incorporate a hammer-wheel and thus to supersede Race II, its siting, with a finery incorporated, is a possible guide to an earlier layout, with furnaces occupying the east of the site, presumably powered by a race, obliterated by later work. A fragment of a roof truss in layer 8C, and tiles and slate in 7F suggest that some of the site at least had been roofed (see Appendix).

The documents show that the forge could just have been built before the blast furnace (pp. 29–36) was abandoned, possibly with the intention of refining its products.

1 D. W. Crossley, 'A 16th-Century Wealden Blast Furnace: excavations at Panningridge Sussex, 1964–70'. *Post-Medieval Archaeology*, 6 (1972), 57–8.

PERIOD III (Figs. 3, 5, 9a, 10, 14, 15; Pls. VA, VII–XI).

In the western part of the site there was a clear break between the equipment ascribed to Period II and a radical rebuilding involving the construction of a race for a single breast-wheel (Figs. 5a and 14). However, in the area to the east there appears to have been a progressive rebuilding over many decades. For convenience Period III is divided into two phases, A and B, and IIIA may not be entirely separable from II. The primary function was to refine pig-iron into bar, with secondary manufacture of a variety of tools.

IIIA   At some time probably in the early seventeenth century the dam associated with Period II, with its clay bank and revetting logs, was elaborated to the east of the Period II race. Wooden piles were driven in front of the dam face, and used to support a stone revetting wall which could also have served as the south wall of a forge building (Fig. 5f). Layer 4P had been used to level up over the original timber revetting beam, but contained no datable finds. The stone was of one build with a well-constructed dry-stone-lined wheel-race running along the eastern edge of the site, in whose silts and associated working levels was found seventeenth-century pottery. This race was built in a trench (Figs. 5a and 5d) cut into natural, and filled, behind the masonry, with sand and clay (layers 2F and 7D). It discharged into an ill-defined tailrace, in which attempts at revetment had been made by laying cinder hearth-bottoms along either side of the channel. The race was aligned directly towards the ditch surviving along the eastern side of the field.

The original purpose of this race appears to have been twofold. Aligned to correspond with this part of the race was a fulcrum-post (Fig. 14; Pl. VIIIA) constructed of re-used timbers, for a tilt hammer. Its position, both in terms of distance and alignment, makes it unlikely in the extreme that it was related to any of the western races, whereas it was close to, and its foundation parallel with the stone race. It is likely that a water wheel had been mounted close to the dam head, and that a short shaft had operated a tail-helve hammer mounted on the fulcrum. It is highly probable that an overshot wheel had been employed for there was no shaped stone breast at the back of the wheel-pit (Pl. VII), as might have been expected if a pitch-back or breast-wheel had been used. The surviving anvil base did not align with the fulcrum (Fig. 15) and must have been a later feature; however, the eastern side of the main anvil pit contained a shelf (Fig. 5a), probably the vestiges of the pit for an earlier hammer. The pottery from the lower part of the build-up of working debris in this area suggests an early seventeenth-century date for construction.

Further north the stone-lined race had been culverted by stone slabs supported on corbels (Fig. 5d). Alongside this covered length a small building had been erected on the west side of the race. Only four courses of stone and brick survived, and it had apparently been patched and rebuilt in stone and in brick on numerous occasions. It contained (Figs. 5d, 14) the vestiges of a finery hearth, originally lined with iron plates and an adjacent pit, probably for cinder from the fining process.[1] Traces of the

---

[1] H. R. Schubert, 'The Early Refining of Pig Iron in England', *Transactions of the Newcomen Society*, 28 (1951–3), 59–75.

C

plates (Pl. VII) had survived as lines of crusts of corrosion, being clearest on the west, far, side of the field-drain trench. They were not found at the eastern end of the hearth, within the surviving area of the building, where the consolidated hearth material 4E marked the outline. The cinder pit had originally occupied most of the south-eastern part of the building, but hard deposits had been allowed to accumulate in its eastern end during the life of the finery. The west end of the building and much of the hearth had been destroyed by a field drain. The culvert stones over the race had provided access to the finery from the rising ground to the east, where the seventeenth-century ground surface was plentifully strewn with charcoal, mostly beech and oak, the fuel for the hearth.

Although no tuyere survived, the bellows for the hearth were found to have been mounted outside the north wall. They had been supported on a timber structure indicated by a group of post-holes, which corresponded with the position of the hearth inside the building. These post-holes thus indicated the position of the bellows wheel, which would almost certainly have been undershot, mounted at the extreme northern end of the race, where culverting was absent.

Thus the eastern race had spaces for two wheels, and it is likely that for a time these had been in simultaneous operation. However, this cannot have been a satisfactory arrangement. Despite the generally excellent construction and cleanly-built sides and bottom of the race, its gradient (1 in 65) was so slight that tail-water from the overshot hammer-wheel would move slowly. The flow would be slowed still further by the operation of an undershot wheel for the finery, which could have caused water to back-up under the first wheel.

This explains the reversion to a race on the western side of the site for the hammer-wheel, discussed under IIIB. When the change took place is not certain, but the material in layer 5F, the lower gritty silt of the eastern race, beneath the culvert capstones, is a guide. This was thick enough to suggest deposit after the IIIA hammer-wheel had been abandoned or removed; yet it was below the final silt (layer 5A) which contained stones and tile fragments, and choked the whole culvert. The latter was apparently deposited after the need for a water-feed to the finery wheel had passed, at the eventual abandonment of the site in the eighteenth century. The pottery in 5F, Flemish stoneware and local red wares, suggest an end-date for this hammer-wheel rather earlier than 1650, and perhaps as early as 1620; the gap in documented use of the site at the time of the Civil War should be borne in mind in this context (p. 4).

IIIB   After IIIA the hammer fulcrum went out of use; either it was cut down or it decayed to ground level and was thus covered over by finery cinder and ash from two small smithing hearths (Fig. 14; Pl. VII) discussed below (p. 27). The anvil pit was enlarged and slightly re-sited (Fig. 5a) to accommodate an anvil block in the position of the one excavated. The frequent replacement of anvil blocks seen in sixteenth-century documents[1] makes it unwise to assume that the one excavated was the original.

At this stage, perhaps late in the seventeenth century and after the break in the documentary record, a return was made to siting a hammer-wheel on the western side

---

[1] See, in particular, references in the De L'Isle MSS (K.A.O.) to Robertsbridge Forge; e.g. U1475 B8/4.

of the forge. The Period II wheel-pit and race were filled in, and a new structure (IIIB) was erected, at a slightly higher level. Due to the stratigraphical break caused by the field drain across the forge floor, it is impossible to be certain about these relationships; for instance it might be argued that the II and IIIA races and hammers were in simultaneous use, or even, that there were, later, hammers being driven from the IIIA and IIIB races at the same time. However, there really was insufficient evidence or indeed room for two anvils in the intervening space to make either proposition seriously tenable.

The IIIB wheel-pit was of 2 in. beech planks set at a gradient of 1:100 between two longitudinal beech timbers each 14–17 in. square,[1] in turn laid on oak sleepers on fill over the silts in the II wheel-pit. As there was relatively little difference in levels between II and IIIB (see Section A–B: Fig. 5a; and Pls. VA, IX), a good deal of rough-and-ready dismantling had been necessary to accommodate the new structure. However, good use was made of the base sleepers of II, for sleepers for IIIB were laid across them, ensuring stability. Thus the layout and strength of II seems to have been clear to the builders of IIIB, who diverged from its layout and alignment to gain a little extra height and, presumably, to employ a different size and type of hammer. This knowledge of II suggests that it cannot have been abandoned for long, and indeed the layers beneath IIIB gave every appearance of a dumped rather than a silted filling, except for 8C, the bottom silt, which was relatively slight.

The three base sleepers were 10 in. × 4–6 in. in section, laid beneath the main wheel-pit beams. There were three further sleepers; one lay towards the dam, to support uprights carrying the top of the wheel-breast: the surface of this south sleeper was rotten and the mortice slots were indistinct. The other two additional sleepers were built into the stonework of the tailrace south of the chafery wheel-pit. In Pl. VA the relationship of the IIIB sleepers, the II base frame and fragments of the I upper frame is apparent. The main lengthwise timbers carried uprights for the breast, penstock and wheel bearings, and on the west timber there were set a regular series of pairs of verticals running down the side of the wheel position. These probably supported the water-feed for the chafery penstock (see below, p. 27). In addition the main timbers had nailed to them the edge-set horizontal boards lining the wheel-pit. Also, nailed to the top of the main eastern long timber was a smaller longitudinal member, 6 × 6 in. in section, morticed to take uprights. To the outside of the west long beam were nailed further edge-set horizontals, so that on this side the wheel-pit had, in effect, a two-skin casing. It was not really obvious why this was necessary, except as part of the support for a chafery supply trough. The beech base of the wheel-pit was made up of pairs of planks, with horse and cow-hair caulking, nailed to the bottom sleepers. The breast was a continuation of this, curving up to the level of the water table, where it had decayed (Pl. IX). Assuming a consistent clearance between breast and wheel of 2 in., common in eighteenth-century practice, a wheel 11 ft 4 in. in diameter could have been used. No fragments remained from which this estimate could be verified. Two lines of small posts ran between the breast and the dam (see p. 28 below), to carry a penstock or water-shoot to the wheel.

[1] See Appendix, p. 40.

Figure 14 and Pl. VIIIB show the timbers which lay between the wheel-pit and the anvil. These were the foundations for the hammer, whose helve must have lain parallel with the spindle, the latter operating a tappet at either the tail or the belly. The probable line of the wheel-spindle was so close to the projected centre-line of the anvil that a tail-helve hammer seems the more likely. A belly helve would require the wheel-spindle to be set to the side of the hammer fulcrum, while with a tail-helve, pivoted at its centre, the cam wheel need only be slightly offset, that is, by the radius of the cam wheel.

The anvil foundation was a remarkably substantial assembly, and does much to explain the expenditure of labour recorded on replacements in accounts for forges in the Weald. The pit itself, 6 ft 6 in. deep, was an enlargement and re-siting of those of earlier periods; in the bottom were timbers laid on the natural sand and sandstone,

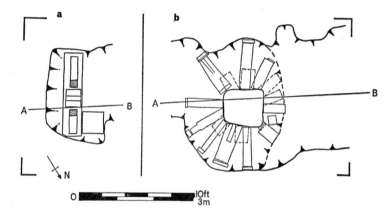

Fig. 15.   Fulcrum post and pit; anvil braces; position indicated on Fig. 14

but these were less regular than the contemporary half-jointed cruciform base at Rockley (Yorks.).[1] Upon this base had been set a length of oak tree-trunk 7 ft long, standing on end. In the upper half of the pit there had been set radial timbers, wedged between the block and verticals placed against the edge of the pit (Fig. 15; Pls. XA–B). The filling around these timbers contained no datable objects. Thus steadied, the block appeared to have carried an iron anvil; this had not been left in place, but its base was outlined by an area free of the rusty stain left by hammer-scale.

The working area around the anvil was floored with heavy beams and was covered with ash and cinder. The pottery in these deposits (layers 4B and 4N) was sparse, and none need be earlier than the seventeenth century.

It appears that the finery was in use throughout IIIA and IIIB in substantially the form excavated, and would convert pig-iron into blooms of refined low-carbon iron to be drawn out into bar under the hammer. However, in order for the latter to be done, a further re-heating hearth, the chafery, was required. The fragmentary foundations of

[1] D. W. Crossley and D. Ashurst, 'Excavations at Rockley Smithies', Post-Medieval Archaeology, 2 (1968), 28–9.

a chafery were recorded north-west of the anvil and adjacent to the tailrace of IIIb. This had been a square stone hearth with an ashpit on the east side, with the clay within and surrounding the hearth reddened by heat. On the north side were post-holes indicating a bellows foundation. In the form excavated, this hearth had been blown using power from a water-wheel set in the IIIb tailrace. Whether it had been sited here or powered in this way earlier than IIIb was not clear: it could have been driven from the finery wheel shaft, although the latter would have needed to be at least 25 ft long to reach across the site. There were no stratified objects to assist the dating of the chafery hearth.

The chafery wheel (Figs. 9a and 14; Pl. XIb) was overshot and caulked with calf-hair; it was 1 ft 11 in. in internal width and 8 ft in diameter, and mounted in a chamber offset from the stone-lined length of the IIIb tailrace; the chamber had been built with a stone floor 8 in. higher than the bottom of the hammer tailrace adjacent, and was separated from it by edge-set horizontal timbers. These had not survived, but the pairs of wooden piles driven along the eastern edge of the flagged floor appeared to be set to hold such a barrier, designed to prevent water from the hammer-wheel reaching the chafery pit. The feed to the chafery wheel must have been overhead, and had not survived. It could well have been a trough mounted on the vertical timbers tenoned to the western long member of the hammer wheel-pit, and described above. The size and position of these members is not otherwise easy to explain.

The stone tailrace ran beyond the excavated area, but trial trenching showed that it ended between 8 and 14 ft north of section C–D (Fig. 2). It had been constructed after the completion of the timber race for the hammer-wheel, but not necessarily as a separate operation. The silts in the stone part of the tailrace produced quantities of finds from the last period of use and the decay of the site. Layer 7S (Fig. 5b) was of great interest, containing Fulham stoneware, not produced before 1671, and a variety of metal objects. These are fully considered below (pp. 61–84), but it should be made clear here that there were sufficient groups of similar objects, particularly scissor fragments, to suggest that in IIIb the site was also being used for smithing and secondary metal working. Indeed, the silting of the IIIb tailrace during the deposition of these objects indicates that the hammer and chafery wheels were only infrequently in use, a point supported by the low annual production of bar iron recorded in 1717 (p. 5).

The presence of material of this kind emphasizes the significance of the pair of small hearths (Fig. 14) referred to above (p. 24). These, lying to the south of the finery hearth, overlay deposits of forge cinder and were built late in IIIb. They survived as rings of vitrified stone fused into cinder and bricks. They could have served for heating blades and small objects, but were too small to act as chaferies. There was no evidence that they had been blown by water-powered bellows nor would their size make this likely. In addition, west of the IIIb wheel-pit there had been set a small anvil, resting on clumsily grouped scrap timbers (Pl. XIa), which bore the outline of an anvil block, surrounded by metal hammer-scale. Neither its position nor its form made it seem a suitable base for a power hammer, and it must be presumed to have been used at a late stage for hand forging.

The dam for Period III followed the line of II. It may have been higher, for close to the forge it was strengthened by the addition of stonework referred to above (p. 23), and behind the IIIB penstock a substantial timber had been set in a bed of red clay unique on the site, apparently to steady the dam material. However, the levelling of the site between 1759 and 1813 had removed all indication of the dam height. The IIIA race and the chafery wheel in IIIB had probably been fed over their full height; as the latter wheel was 8 ft in diameter its feed would have had to be at least 4 ft higher than the modern ground surface, giving an idea of the minimum height of the dam (Fig. 10). The IIIB breast-wheel, on the other hand, had been fed at a lower level, through a channel cut through the II dam (section E–F, Fig. 5c).

There was some evidence that in IIIB at least, and probably IIIA, the whole complex had been under a roof. There were fragments of roof-timbers in the build-up for IIIB, and the stone wall along the face of the dam, originating in IIIA, suggested the kind of back wall seen at the forge at Wortley (Yorkshire), built at the beginning of the eighteenth century. The demolition layer covering the whole working area contained tiles among stone and cinder, and the evennness of the spread suggests that a roof had covered much or all the ground between the two races. In IIIB, indeed, a roof may have gone further west, for a prominent sill-beam (Fig. 14; Pl. XIA) lay 12 ft beyond the IIIB race, limiting the working debris 7Q (Fig. 5a) west of the small hand anvil. The northerly extent was less easy to establish, but the otherwise inexplicable post-holes north of the chafery-finery area could well have supported the roof on an open north side.

This does appear to be a relatively complete picture of the works. Machine-trenches were dug at intervals across the field to the west, extending downstream into possible working areas. Despite the limitations of this form of testing, which time and resources made the only possible approach, no sign of any other working site was seen. Surface indications had suggested other channels on the downstream side of the dam; one was excavated over a limited area (see p. 14 above), producing no clear dating evidence, and only an inference that an early channel, perhaps even the original course of the Bewl had given rise to persistent damp conditions. A patch of ill-drained ground also ran to the north-west of the area stripped, to the west of the I–II–IIIB races. This however contained no evidence of structures and was no more than a shallow cinder-filled depression, perhaps an overflow from the medieval stream bed.

The site since its abandonment

The subsequent history is of interest not only because certain features were utilized during improvement of the neighbouring land, but because this activity, involving the cutting of drains resulting in a high water table, aiding the survival and interpretation of timbers.

It is not entirely certain when the pond was drained. It is shown on the Scotney estate map of 1828, but as this is a re-use (see p. 7, note 1) of a survey of 1759 it is uncertain whether all features were revised.[1] The first edition Ordnance Survey map (1813) does not show the pond, so it must have been drained between 1759 and 1813. Afterwards the hollow in which the forge lay acted as a focus for the layout of field drains. The tailrace, leading to the Bewl, encouraged this, and water was fed in from

[1] See p. 5, note 5; and p. 7, note 1.

the hillside to the east through an open ditch to a stone collecting drain laid (Section G–H; Fig. 5d) directly on top of the culverting stones of the IIIA race, and thence discharging into the silted finery wheel-pit. A prominent stone drain, similarly with squared side-stones and top slabs, was laid across the anvil pit to the IIIA tailrace (Fig. 5d). Perhaps significantly this only began at the dam, although subsequently a pipe drain had been linked to it there (Fig. 5e). It is thus possible that the stone drains were built at a time when something remained of the dam.

Straker quotes the late Mr E. W. Hussey that cinder was dug about 1840. It may well be that the upper parts of the dam had been built and rebuilt with cinder, as was not uncommon in the Weald, and that the remains had been removed and levelled at this time. There was a great quantity of mixed cinder and clay spread northwards over the site from the dam, and the pipe drains extending back through the dam area into the pond field would be consistent with a final levelling at about this time.

CHINGLEY FURNACE

The site was essentially of one period, and although the furnace structure had been rebuilt, the plan had not been altered. The modifications that were identified during the excavation are dealt with in the descriptions of individual features.

The builders had chosen a point where the valley narrowed, to allow a short dam. In 1972 this survived, except where breached by the Bewl (Fig. 16), to a height of 8 ft above the ground on either side. Immediately downstream from the northern end of the dam the hillslope at the foot of Chingley Wood had been steeply scarped away. This created a platform in the side of the valley, on which were built the furnace, its bellows-house and at some point during the life of the site, a lean-to outbuilding. The wheel-pit and tailrace had been cut along the southern edge of the platform.[1]

The Furnace (Figs. 16–18; Pls. XII–XVI) had been a stone tower 18 ft square, its base built on a platform of weathered sandstone without foundation trenches apart from a slight depression along the western side. The bottom course was well built, with ashlar outer faces and a core of rubble. A further three and in places four courses of outer stonework survived, but these were of poorer construction, using smaller stones which bulged out along the north and west wall-faces.[2] The contrast was emphasized by the core, which at this level was of clay. A foundation trench (Fig. 18b) had been dug outside the north and west walls in order to build the replacement stonework; this had been cut into debris which had accumulated over the back drain (p. 35 below).

The pillar of the furnace, separating the blowing and casting arches, had a maximum of five surviving courses, the bottom two of which were of substantial stones, the rest small and badly laid. The furnace had a timber bracing: at each corner was a small inset

[1] For a wider discussion of the features of sixteenth-century blast furnaces, reference should be made to the report on the excavated site at Panningridge (Crossley, 1972).

[2] Some re-used stone seems to have been employed in the upper part of the structure: a fragment of a mullion was found in the demolition debris near the furnace pillar; this had come from a building of high-quality construction. It is not impossible that stone may have been sold off from Bayham Abbey (TQ 649365) at this time.

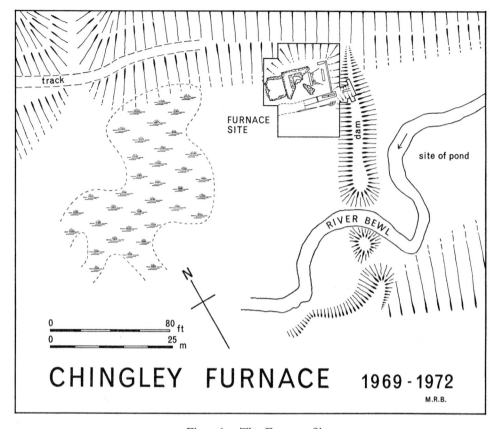

Fig. 16.   The Furnace Site

for a vertical post, and bases of these timbers survived, each 10–12 in. square, except at the south-east corner. They had been placed on the surface, without post-holes or stylobates.

The hearth (Figs. 17 and 18c; Pl. XIII) had survived sufficiently to give an indication of its original size. The southern half, over the casting aperture, had disappeared when the furnace superstructure was robbed. The northern half was intact, and provided a section through the lining and the accumulated slag; the lining had been badly scabbed with slag during the final campaign, and its dimensions can only be approximately deduced.[1] The hearth had been built within a stone-lined chamber which survived to 4 ft 6 in. above the surface of the platform; full use had not been made of the available space at the last re-lining, for the northern part of the chamber, behind the lining stones,

---

[1] Figure 18c gives some impression of the build-up. It was not possible to be certain where lining ended and slag began in the section, but the best estimate of the original diameter of the hearth (and it seems as likely to have been round as square in plan) was about 2 ft 9 in. to 3 ft 3 in. It had been reduced by slag to about 2 ft (east–west, Section E–F in Fig. 18c), and by perhaps rather less from north–south, to judge by the plan. This might be the point when a campaign would no longer be worth continuing.

CHINGLEY FURNACE

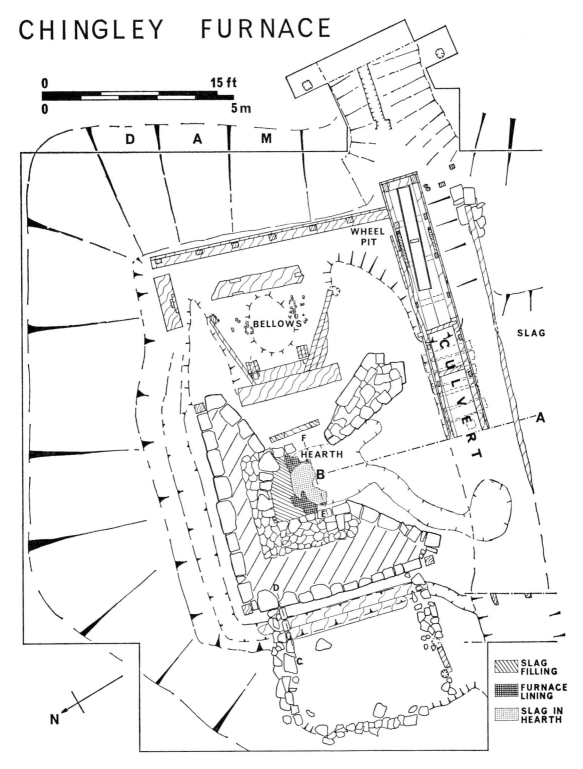

0   15 ft

0   5 m

D A M

WHEEL PIT

BELLOWS

SLAG

CULVERT

A

F

HEARTH

B

E

D

C

N

SLAG FILLING

FURNACE LINING

SLAG IN HEARTH

Fig. 17. The Furnace: plan of excavation

had been filled with slag. Indeed, seen in plan, this last hearth appears south of centre. Fragments survived of the replaceable blocking of the tuyere arch, inserted at each re-lining. Beneath the hearth was a drain, covered by the roughly-vaulted bottom stones of the lining. This was a depression dug into the natural material, with two channels running southwards; the westerly reached the tailrace, the other was incomplete. The western channel had been sharply cut into the slag covering of the culverted tailrace, filled with a porous mixture of sand and large slag lumps, and sealed by the slag and sand of the casting floor. It thus seems likely that this drainage soak-away was an addition, particularly as the hollow under the hearth did not underly any of the furnace masonry. The need could be explained by the choking and decay of the furnace backdrain, perhaps failing to remove water from the springs at the edge of the platform. It did seem possible, early in the excavation, that the drain pit could have been intended for gun-casting, but apart from the absence of any mould material or timber lining, its connexion with the channel from under the hearth made drainage the better explanation.

The casting floor bore no traces of pig-beds or moulds, although a layer of sand 3–6 in. thick covered the area within the casting arch and south to the kerb edging the slag heap. Beneath this layer traces of sand appeared in the slag filling over the tailrace, emphasizing that smelting had initially taken place with a small casting floor within the arch, providing slag and used sand for the filling. Unused sand was piled near the south-east corner of the furnace.

The Bellows area. A sill-beam was set at the foot of the dam, with tenoned uprights and a back wall of edge-set horizontal planks. This formed the eastern wall of the bellows house, whose roof would be fixed at its western side to the wall of the furnace, over the blowing arch. Within, a trapezoid hollow (Fig. 17) 12–15 in. deep, contained traces of two sets of bellows. The two pivot posts[1] survived intact, with holes of 1 in. diameter for the bearing pins. The timber had worn in use, and new holes had been cut once in the east post, and twice in the western. The posts were held by iron stirrups (Fig. 43, no. 4) to a horizontal beam set in the western edge of the hollow, and notched to provide clearance for the main lengthwise timbers of the bellows bottom boards. The northern notch was well preserved, the southern rotten and barely discernible. The northern and southern edges of the hollow were held by horizontal timbers laid from the front beam to the vertical posts. The front of the bellows and the tuyere pipes had lain on beams set on the main platform. The smaller of these timbers, close to the furnace, had slots to take the pipes. The large beam would support the front of the bellows boxes. Within the hollow were numerous wedges, driven into the surface in clumps. Their purpose is not certain, unless to prevent the lower board of the bellows falling and scraping the back of the camshaft between lifts. The bellows-house floor was covered with fragments of leather and timber, and nails with broad heads (Fig. 45, no. 13) from repeated re-covering and patching of the bellows. The natural sands were discoloured purple by the leather to a depth of 2–4 in.

[1] North post: 12 × 10 in.; south post: 13 × 11 in.

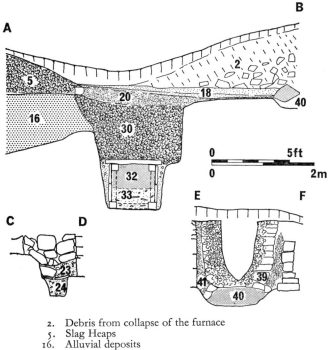

2. Debris from collapse of the furnace
5. Slag Heaps
16. Alluvial deposits
18. Casting sand
20. Fine cinder and slag
23. Filling of rebuilding trench ⎱
24. Filling of foundation trench ⎰ West of furnace
30. Coarse slag and cinder
32. Fine silt within tailrace culvert
33. Silt and vegetation debris
39. Furnace lining, with slag adhering
40. Silt in furnace under-drain
41. Slag filling between furnace and hearth stones

Fig. 18.   The Furnace: sections

A fragment of the oak camshaft had fallen from the operating height indicated by
the oak bearing block to the north.[1] Sufficient remained to show that the shaft had
at least two sets of three cams. These were staggered, so that with the two sets of
bellows there would be blast every 60 degrees of rotation of the shaft. It is probable
that the bottom rather than the top boards of the bellows were hinged, as the pivots
were set low relative to tuyere level. The boards could have been raised directly by the
cams as shown by Birringuccio,[2] a system which required long and therefore very
strong cams and housings; alternatively a system of overhead levers could have been

[1] The block (Pl. XVI), 15 in. high, 17 in. wide and 54 in. long, had a semi-circular cut-out of 19 in. radius
and 6 in. deep to clear the end of the shaft, and a rectangular housing 8 × 4 in. in plan and 3 in. deep to take
a bearing. Thus the shaft probably had a rod hammered into its end, which would run in the bearing. Agicola's
illustrations in Book IX of *De Re Metallica* make the most likely arrangement clear.
[2] Biringuccio, fig. 47, p. 301.

used, supported on the available upright posts, as illustrated by Agricola[1] who shows hinges at the top rather than the bottom. However hinged bottom boards would not be incompatible with an overhead lever system.

The part of the overshot water-wheel beneath the level of the water table had survived; it was set in a timber-lined wheel-pit and, beyond it, to the south, lay scattered stones from the support for the shaft bearing. The wheel was 11 ft 2 in. in overall diameter, and 9 ft 7 in. in diameter to the outside of the sole board. Its buckets were 10 in. wide between 1-1½ in. thick side boards. The bucket boards were 1-1½ in. thick, curved, and fastened to the sides with nails; they were further held in position by 1 in. diameter dowels resting against their convex back surfaces and set in holes in the side boards. One spoke survived intact to within 6 in. of the centre line of the wheel. Its tenon was placed through a hole in the sole board, and a rectangular wooden cotter was fixed through a mortice-slot in the spoke, on the outside of the sole. This was not the first wheel to be used, for fragments of straight bucket boards lay in the lower silt of the wheel-pit.

The wheel-pit had a floor of 1 in. planks[2] pegged by 1 in. diameter dowels to cross-sleepers (3 × 5 in.) beneath; the three cross-sleepers were half-jointed to the long members. The frame of the pit was made up of base longitudinal members, 6 × 5 in., side uprights (shown in plan in Fig. 17) 2½ × 5 in., and rear corner posts 9½ × 7 in. The upper long members were less substantial, the one to the north was badly twisted, and both had partly rotted; their section appears to have been 5 × 5 in. The side and end boards, of 1 in. oak planking set on edge, were placed behind the uprights. The rear corner posts were morticed to the adjacent members; the side uprights were morticed at their bases and half-jointed at the top. Two members set at 45 degrees and providing penstock supports shared a mortice slot with adjacent uprights (Fig. 17). Apart from the wheel fragments, the lower silts contained pottery, scraps of leather and a bloom of wrought iron (p. 58) amongst vegetation and pieces of timber. The upper silts were finer, the result of gradual accumulation after abandonment.

The wheel had been fed from a penstock laid high on the dam. Figure 17 shows a beam-slot across the dam, probably holding a supporting sleeper for the water-feed, and a post-hole on either side.[3] The rest of the dam-top was disturbed by roots. Posts to support the front of the penstock were built into the wheel-pit; those marked on Fig. 17 had clearly been longer than the rest of the verticals, also four posts were recorded immediately to the south of the head of the wheel-pit.

The tailrace formed an unfloored continuation of the wheel-pit, using the same sections of oak for sleepers, lengthwise horizontals, and sideboards, with better-preserved material for the upper members. In addition 12 × 2½ in. boards were placed over the channel; this had then been covered in, using slag presumably produced during an early campaign of the furnace. This formed the southern part of the casting floor, over which casting sand was spread. The culvert was almost completely silted; a lower level containing vegetation, pot sherds and fragments of wood was probably deposited

[1] Agricola, p. 359.
[2] The north plank was 12¾ in. wide, the south 14¾ in. All the timbers in the pit were oak.
[3] The difference in height between the floor of the wheel-pit and the apparent level of the floor of the water-feed trough was 13 ft 6 in., corresponding well with the 11 ft 2 in. diameter of the wheel.

during or soon after the use of the furnace, while above it was a fine silt, the result of long seepage over the succeeding centuries.

The western end of the culvert lay beyond the south-west corner of the furnace: it discharged into an unrevetted channel between scarped natural sand on the north side and the valley-bottom alluvium to the south. It was not feasible to excavate the entire length of the culvert due to instability of this alluvium under the weight of the overlying slag deposits which covered the centre of the valley. Some attempt had been made to hold these away from the furnace by a slight timber kerb which marked the southward extent of the casting floor.

Into the open tailrace, immediately to the west of the culvert, there discharged a back-drain which had been cut outside the northern and western walls of the furnace. This had tapped springs exposed by the scarping of the hillside, although a good deal of water must have leaked eastwards and then across the bellows-house floor. The drain was filled with porous ash and covered by boards, but it must soon have been forgotten. Not only had debris piled over the boards, to be cut through by the rebuilding-trench for the furnace (above, p. 29) but the north and south walls of the outhouse had been built across the drain, the stones collapsing into it (Fig. 18: c-d).

The outhouse was probably the final structure to be built, for its stones were set against the new upper courses of the west walls of the furnace. It had a doorway 2 ft 6 in.-3 ft wide in the south wall, a fragment of the wooden threshold being in position with a post-hole at its west end, and a possible equivalent to the east. There were no traces of ore or charcoal, which would in any case be more likely to be stored at the far end of a charging bridge, and the doorway, if it were the only one, would be awkwardly narrow for sows of cast iron, particularly with the edge of the open tailrace so close.

The only element missing on this site was a charging bridge. This would be vital for a furnace perhaps 15–18 ft in height, but easily provided from the high ground to the north. Little trace would be left of what need have been no more than a planked barrow-run.[1]

The abandonment of the site.   The reference to the decay of the furnace by 1588 (p. 4, note 2) was supported by the lack of any pottery of seventeenth-century character, or of clay pipes. There was thus no reason to suppose that the furnace was re-started by Richard Ballard when he took over Thomas Dyke's lease in 1597. The time of robbing could not be established, as no dating evidence came from the collapsed debris. It would be reasonable to suggest that ashlar from the superstructure was re-used in the development of the forge (Period IIIA) early in the seventeenth century.

The most notable aspect of the site was its compact layout. The furnace was built as close as possible to the hillside, given the need for an outside drain, and the culverted tailrace was a particularly adroit means of reducing the length of the wheel shaft, by bringing the water-wheel as close as possible to the furnace. This does indeed raise the question of how common this layout was, for at Panningridge, Sussex, there were indications of an impracticably small casting floor close to a tailrace early in the life of

[1] That the storage area for raw materials was remote from the furnace was emphasized by the lack of charcoal or ore in the excavated area.

the furnace. This could have been usable, if carried over the adjacent channel in a manner similar to Chingley.[1]

It is not possible to associate the rebuilding of the furnace with any documented change of tenancy. The only change known is that of 1579, and although major work could have been done by Thomas Dyke in that year, there is nothing against an earlier or later date.

[1] Crossley, 1972, 49, n. 8.

IV   Appendix

THE MEASUREMENT OF TIMBERS AND JOINTS AT THE FORGE[1]

PERIOD I

(numbering of lower beams corresponds with Fig. 4, p. 9,
of upper beams with Fig. 6, p. 11)

The base members

Cross sleepers S, V, Y $13\frac{3}{4} \times 7\frac{7}{8}$

Long sleepers

T $9\frac{7}{8} > 9\frac{1}{2} \times 5\frac{1}{8} > 4\frac{1}{2}$ Section;   Tenon with S $9\frac{1}{2} \times 1\frac{3}{4}$; 4 long.
 Tenon with V $7\frac{1}{4} \times 2\frac{1}{2}$; $3\frac{3}{4}$.

U $9\frac{5}{8} > 9\frac{1}{2} \times 4\frac{3}{4}$ Section;   Tenon with S $9\frac{1}{4} \times 1\frac{3}{4}$; $2\frac{3}{8}$.
 Dovetail V $4\frac{3}{8} < 5\frac{1}{8} \times 1\frac{3}{8} > \frac{3}{4}$; $3\frac{1}{2}$.

W $10\frac{1}{2} > 7\frac{1}{2} \times 5\frac{1}{8} > 4\frac{1}{2}$ Section;   Tenon V $6\frac{7}{8} \times 1\frac{3}{4}$; $3\frac{3}{8}$.
 Tenon Y $8\frac{5}{8} \times 1\frac{3}{4}$; $3\frac{1}{2}$.

X $9 > 7\frac{1}{4} \times 5\frac{1}{2}$ Section;   Tenon V $7\frac{1}{8} \times 1\frac{1}{2}$; $3\frac{3}{4}$.
 Tenon Y $8\frac{5}{8} \times 2$; $3\frac{3}{4}$.

Verticals	Section	Tenon section	Tenon length
A1	$12\frac{1}{2} \times 12\frac{1}{2}$	$12\frac{1}{2} \times 2\frac{1}{2}$	4
A2	$15\frac{1}{2} \times 12$	$15\frac{1}{2} \times 2\frac{1}{2} > 2\frac{1}{4}$	$3\frac{3}{4}$
A3	$13 \times 12\frac{1}{2}$	$12\frac{1}{2} \times 2\frac{1}{2} > 2\frac{1}{4}$	$4\frac{1}{8}$
A4	$14\frac{1}{2} \times 11\frac{1}{4}$	$13\frac{3}{8} \times 2\frac{3}{4} > 2\frac{1}{4}$	$3\frac{3}{4}$
A5	$14\frac{1}{4} \times 11\frac{1}{2}$	(unobtainable)[2]	
B1	$13 \times 11\frac{1}{2}$	$12\frac{3}{4} \times 2\frac{1}{4}$	4
B2	$16 \times 12\frac{3}{4}$	$15\frac{3}{4} \times 2\frac{1}{2}$	4
B3	$10\frac{3}{4} \times 10\frac{3}{4}$	$10\frac{5}{8} \times 2\frac{1}{4}$	4
B4	$8\frac{5}{8} \times 9$	$8\frac{5}{8} \times 2\frac{1}{4}$	4
B5	$13\frac{3}{8} \times 12$	$11 \times 2\frac{1}{4}$	4
C1	$12\frac{1}{2} \times 12$	$12\frac{1}{2} \times 2\frac{1}{2}$	4
C2	$15\frac{3}{4} \times 12\frac{1}{4}$	$15\frac{3}{4} \times 2\frac{1}{2}$	4
C3	$14\frac{1}{2} \times 11\frac{1}{2}$	$14\frac{1}{2} \times 2\frac{1}{2}$	4
C4	$8\frac{5}{8} \times 11\frac{1}{2}$	$8\frac{5}{8} \times 2\frac{1}{2}$	$3\frac{3}{4}$
C5	$15\frac{1}{2} \times 10\frac{1}{4}$	$13 \times 2\frac{1}{4}$	4
D1		(2×7)	
D2	missing	(2×8)	
D3		$(2 \times 7\frac{1}{2})$[3]	
D4	$5\frac{1}{2} \times 6\frac{1}{4}$	$2 \times 6\frac{1}{4}$	$3\frac{1}{2}$
D5	$5 \times 7\frac{1}{4}$	$1\frac{7}{8} \times 7\frac{1}{4}$	$3\frac{1}{2}$

[1] All measurements are in inches. The east-west dimension precedes the north-south in the case of sections through vertically-set timbers; the vertical precedes the horizontal in sections through horizontal timbers. In all cases the length of a timber, tenon, etc., is placed last.

[2] Unstable ground prevented the safe removal of A5.

[3] Where the tenon was missing the (larger) mortice dimension is given in brackets.

Verticals	Section	Tenon section	Tenon length
D6	$6\frac{1}{2} \times 6\frac{7}{8}$	$1\frac{7}{8} \times 6\frac{1}{2}$	$3\frac{3}{4}$
E1	$5\frac{1}{4} \times 6\frac{3}{4}$	$1\frac{7}{8} \times 6\frac{3}{4}$	$3\frac{1}{2}$
E2	$6\frac{1}{4} \times 8\frac{1}{4}$	$1\frac{7}{8} \times 8\frac{1}{4}$	$3\frac{1}{2}$
E3	$6\frac{3}{4} \times 6\frac{3}{4}$	$1\frac{7}{8} \times 6\frac{3}{4}$	$3\frac{3}{4}$
E4	$5 \times 6\frac{1}{8}$	$1\frac{7}{8} \times 6\frac{1}{8}$	$3\frac{1}{2}$
E5	$6 \times 7\frac{1}{2}$	$1\frac{7}{8} \times 7\frac{1}{2}$	$3\frac{1}{2}$
E6	$5\frac{1}{2} \times 6$	$1\frac{7}{8} \times 6$	$3\frac{1}{2}$

Upper Cross Beams	Section
S	$12\frac{1}{4} \times 15$
V	12×15
Y	12×15

Surviving Joints on S (upper)

		East (P)	Central (R)	West
Lapped dovetails:	vertical overlap	$2\frac{1}{2}$	$6+$	$4+$ (rotten)
	width at mouth	8	$10\frac{1}{2}$	10
	width at rear	12	$13\frac{1}{4}$	—
	depth to rear	9	9	—
	rear of joint to back of beam	$5\frac{3}{4}$	6	—

Perhaps the most striking parallel for the Period I base frame is the foundation for the bridge at Bodiam Castle.[1] While there are detailed differences, and the dimensions there are altogether more massive, the mortice and half-joints bear an immediate visual resemblance, and although the date of building, c. 1385, is perhaps later than at Chingley, the significance of such a similar approach to design only eight miles away needs little emphasis.

The joints in the Period I structure may also be compared with dated examples from East Anglia. The base frame joints, with their pegged central tenons are typical of the practice of c. 1300, and onwards towards the middle of the fifteenth century. They contrast with the trend towards bare-faced tenons or the more complex variants illustrated by Mr Hewett, which seem, on balance, to be concentrated rather later. The lap-dovetails in the upper joints are typical of practice from 1300 onwards where any form of tying was required. The degrees of set of the dovetails from the long axis of the timber 1:4½ (east joint) and 1:6½ (central joint) illustrate the problems of using this feature for dating. While Hewett[2] has found that in East Anglia the angle is apt to become less over the period 1300–1700, here we have a considerable divergence between adjacent joints. The only dovetail in the base-frame, linking beams U and V is indeed much less angular, at 1:9.

Period II
(numbering corresponding with Fig. 11, p. 18)

Sleepers		*Upper horizontals*	
North–South:	25, $6\frac{1}{2} \times 9\frac{1}{2}$	North–South:	13, $7\frac{3}{8} \times 8$
	26, $6\frac{1}{4} \times 9\frac{1}{2}$		14, $9 \times 10\frac{3}{4}$

[1] D. Martin, *Bodiam Castle Medieval Bridges*, Hastings Area Archaeol. Papers 1 (1973), pp. 4–10.
[2] C. A. Hewett, *The Development of Carpentry 1200–1700: an Essex Study* (Newton Abbot, 1969), pp. 188–204.

Sleepers		*Upper horizontals*
East–West:	22, $6 \times 9\frac{1}{2}$	15, 10×11
	23, $7\frac{1}{4} \times 9$	16, 10×10
	24, $8\frac{1}{2} \times 10\frac{1}{2}$	17, $7\frac{1}{2} \times 11\frac{1}{4}$
		27, 10×8
		28, 7×6
		29, 8×6
	East–West:	20, 10×10
		21, $12 \times 12\frac{3}{4}$

All horizontals were half-jointed at the lower level; 22 and 23 were carried over 25 and 26 (North–South), but 24 was set beneath them. At the upper level, surviving horizontals were again half-jointed with the upper members (north–south),[1] in all cases having their top surfaces standing proud of the upper surface of the east–west members, by amounts varying between $\frac{1}{2}$ in. and 2 in.; 14, 15, 16, and 17 were connected, respectively, to the rear verticals 1, 2, 3, and 5 by horizontal tenons set in mortice slots in the verticals, which had originally been higher. The tenons were generally uniform: 10 in. (vertical), $3\frac{1}{2}$ in. thick, with lengths of $4\frac{1}{4}$ in. (14), $5\frac{1}{4}$ in. (15), $4\frac{1}{2}$ in. (16); however, 17 was $7\frac{1}{2}$ in. wide, 3 in. thick and 4 in. long.

Verticals	Section	lower tenon	upper tenon
1	$12\frac{3}{4} \times 8\frac{1}{4}$	$10\frac{5}{8} (12)^2 \times 2\frac{1}{4} \times 3$	—
2	$12\frac{1}{2} \times 8\frac{1}{4}$	$10 \times 2 \times 3\frac{1}{2}$	—
3	$11\frac{3}{4} \times 10$	$11 \times 2\frac{1}{4} \times 3\frac{1}{2}$	—
4	10×9	$10 \times 2 \times 3\frac{1}{2}$	none surviving
5	$10\frac{1}{2} \times 9$	$6\frac{1}{2} \times 2 \times 3\frac{1}{2}$	—
6	$13 \times 8\frac{1}{2}$	$9\frac{1}{2} \times 2 \times 4$	$10\frac{1}{2} \times 2 \times 3$
7	$13 \times 9\frac{3}{4}$	$11 \times 2 \times 4\frac{1}{4}$	$12 \times 1\frac{3}{4} \times 3$
8	$12\frac{1}{2} \times 9$	$9\frac{1}{2} \times 2 \times 4$	$11 \times 1\frac{3}{4} \times 3\frac{1}{2}$
9	$10\frac{1}{2} \times 8\frac{1}{2}$	$9\frac{1}{4} \times 2 \times 3\frac{3}{4}$	$10\frac{1}{4} \times 2 \times 3\frac{1}{2}$
9a	10×8	$7\frac{1}{2} \times 2 \times 3\frac{1}{2}$	$8 \times 2 \times 4$
10	$4\frac{1}{4} \times 6\frac{1}{4}$	$1\frac{3}{4} \times 6\frac{1}{4} \times 3\frac{3}{4}$	$1\frac{3}{4} \times 6\frac{1}{4} \times 2\frac{3}{4}$
11	$8 \times 21\frac{3}{4} > 10\frac{1}{2}$	$2\frac{1}{4} \times 18\frac{3}{8} \times 3\frac{1}{4}$	$8 \times 2\frac{1}{4} \times 4$
12	$4 \times 7\frac{1}{2}$	$1\frac{1}{2} (2\frac{1}{4}) \times 7\frac{1}{2} (8) \times 2$	$1\frac{1}{2} \times 7\frac{1}{2} \times 2$

The empty mortices in sleeper 26, from which verticals were missing, corresponded with those in 25. Those in cross-sleeper 24 were equivalent to post 7, $10\frac{3}{8}$ in. by $2\frac{1}{4}$ in., those largely corresponding with 4 and 5 were both $9\frac{1}{4}$ in. by $2\frac{1}{2}$ in.

In the Period II base-frame, pegged central tenons are entirely absent from the horizontals, being replaced by half-joints. However they appear at the south end, where the verticals presumed to support the penstock have mortices to take tenons on the upper north–south beams. Slight shoulders help to take the weight ($\frac{1}{2}$ in.–1 in. wide). This is a peculiar arrangement, and must have relied on the weight and a northward thrust in the penstock structure to prevent the joints opening. The verticals, however, did use tenons, with interesting use of long tenons taken through half-joints (Fig. 13). There is one bare-faced lap-dovetail, at the west end of the south beam, of typical post-medieval character, with a $1:4\frac{3}{4}$ set.

[1] The joint between 13 and 21 varied slightly in having a taper west face, giving in effect a partial lap dovetail.
[2] Where the tenon was a poor fit, the (larger) mortice is given in brackets.

D

The considerable variations between examples in the same structure emphasize the problems of using joints as precise dating material, made more acute by differing rates of innovation in individual localities.[1]

THE ROOF TIMBER

A timber from the Period II level (p. 22) appeared to be a 30-degree brace from a roof. It was however an isolated find and its original provenance must remain uncertain. The brace was at least 6 ft 10 in. long, but the end opposite from the well-preserved polygonal tenon was rotten, and not identifiable as part of a further joint. The brace was $3-3\frac{1}{2}$ in. thick and 9 in. deep. It was halved to form the tenon, which was $4\frac{1}{2}$ in. deep. A $2\frac{1}{2}$ in. equilateral triangle had been cut out of the tip of the tenon, to create the polygon. There were two peg-holes, $\frac{3}{4}$ and $1\frac{1}{4}$ in. in diameter. Mr S. E. Rigold has made the following comment:

The tenon cut with a polygonal end for ease of assembly is a refinement that is not very common. It occurs on the braces to the sole-plates on the moat-bridge at Acton Burnell (Salop)[2] perhaps datable to 1300 or before. The Chingley tenon enters its post or plate at a sharp angle and if there is any significance in the preservation of one end it could be that it is a lower end, i.e., that it is a low-pitched *straight* brace, which is consistent with late sixteenth and early seventeenth-century working of good quality, as in bell-frames.

PERIOD IIIA

(Fig. 15, Pl. VIIIA)   Hammer fulcrum post
            Base member   7 ft 2 in. × 1 ft × 1 ft 2 in.
            Vertical   1 ft 4 in. × 1 ft 5 in. section at base
                   forks   5 in. and $5\frac{1}{2}$ in. thick, with $6\frac{1}{2}$ in. gap
            Braces   5 in. × 4 in. (north); 5 in. × 3 in. (south)

PERIOD IIIB

| Main north–south members | East: | 14 in. × 15 in. | } uneven |
| | West: | 15 in. × 17 in. | |

Sleepers:	1.	south of breast (section J–K)	6 in. × 18 in.
	2.	} beneath wheel-pit	8 > 6 in. × 16 in.
	3.		9 > 5 in. × 15 in.
	4.	north of timber wheel-pit	6 in. × 12 in.
	5.	at widening of race	4 in. × 11 > 7 in.

THE IDENTIFICATION OF TIMBERS

Considerations of space preclude a list of all the identifications made during and after the excavation. Where necessary these have been incorporated in the text, and the full list will be deposited with the finds. Thanks are due to Mrs Dorothy Cleere, Miss Ruth Jones (Department of Ancient History, University of Sheffield) and the late Mr L. F. H. Merton (Department of Botany, University of Sheffield) for identifying samples which defeated the author, and for confirming the identifications he did make.

[1] J. T. Smith, Review of Hewett, op. cit., *Post-Medieval Archaeology*, 4 (1970), 200–1.
[2] D. M. Wilson and D. G. Hurst (eds), 'Medieval Britain in 1962 and 1963', *Medieval Archaeology*, 8 (1964), 272–3.

V   Old Forge Farm[1]

By K. W. E. Gravett

Old Forge Farm, Ticehurst (N.G.R. TQ 679338), is basically timber framed, of two storeys and attics. Now two cottages, it was originally one house, built with a central chimney stack with two flues. It is likely that the door was originally in the centre of the main, west front, in front of the chimney. The downstairs room to the north was the main farm kitchen, the oven being the present totally enclosed space beside the chimney to the east. It is not clear where the original stairs were, but probably they ascended steeply above the oven.

The downstairs room to the south shows signs of having been divided longitudinally into two, since the central ceiling beam is original and has a line of blocked mortices.

Of the two upstairs rooms, only that to the north had a fireplace. The roof is of queen strut type, the principal rafters being notched to take side purlins. The main posts have gunstocks on their heads. The roof construction, plan, and type of floor indicate a date in the middle or the second half of the seventeenth century.

At a later date, perhaps *c.* 1800, the outshot was added to the whole of the back, the stairs improved and the tile hanging added. About this time, or perhaps a little later, the house was divided into two, when the stack at the south end was added, with a protruding oven and brick barrel vault. At the end of the nineteenth century, the front was underpinned in brick and considerable repairs carried out to the roof.

---

[1] Demolished in April 1973. It is hoped that a survey will be published in a projected study of Ticehurst's timber buildings (Information from Mr D. Martin).

VI   The Finds

OBJECTS OF WOOD

THE WATER-WHEELS (Fig. 9a)

Estimates of Power Outputs By DR P. STRANGE

(1)	Chingley Forge	c. 1300–50	1.5 hp.[1]	1.12 kW
(2)	Chingley Furnace	1558–80+	1.2 hp.	0.9 kW
(3)	Chingley Forge: Chafery[2]	c. 1670–1780	1.5 hp.	1.12 kW

Assumed wheel circumferential speed = 3 ft/sec.

In the Period I deposits, in addition to the wheel-fragment noted by Dr Strange above, there were other parts likely to have come from water-wheels. The boards on the east side of the south bay were certainly discarded side-pieces from a wheel or wheels, but their edges were too badly damaged and distorted to give usable measurements for the calculation of radii. There were three pieces:

(1)   The radial width was 15 in. Straight buckets had been pegged and nailed to the sides at $8\frac{1}{2}$ in. pitch. The dowel holes (1 in. diameter) were $4\frac{1}{2}$ in. from the inner edge, and there were nail holes $1\frac{1}{2}$ in. and $3\frac{1}{2}$ in. from the outer edge of the board (measured on the radius). The side had been nailed to its sole board, the nails being $1\frac{1}{4}$ in. from the inner edge of the side board, and $3\frac{1}{4}$ in. apart. The ends of the sector of board were chamfered and had been nailed at the overlap.

(2) and (3)   Badly damaged, but all remaining dimensions and features appeared to correspond with (1).

In layers 8H (Period I working deposit) and 8J (residual material scattered over the silts filling the race) immediately to the east of the wheel, were what appeared to be fragments of spokes, in pairs. These were of circular-section oak, $2\frac{1}{2}$–3 in. in diameter, connected by dowels 1–$1\frac{1}{4}$ in. in diameter and surviving up to 16 in. long. The dowels were set in pairs 2–$2\frac{1}{2}$ in. apart, with spaces of 16 in. between pairs. These spacings made it unlikely that the fragments could be part of a ladder, and double spokes from a relatively wide wheel, with dowels to hold them from springing together or apart is offered as a possible, but not a firm explanation. The parallels for double spokes in Agricola (e.g. p. 189) lack the linking dowels.

---

[1] This wheel has been dealt with in the same way as (2) and (3), although the small number of buckets would almost certainly result in a somewhat, c. 10–20%, lower figure for the output power.

[2] This wheel was caulked with a pitch-like material, with fibres adhering (see report, p. 27). Mr J. Evans, North-East London Polytechnic, reports:

Infra-red analysis of this sample, which was insoluble in normal organic solvents, suggested the presence of some organic material. Elemental analysis for carbon, hydrogen and nitrogen accounted for only 10% (by weight) and the residual ash for another 40%. Further work indicated that the remaining bulk was largely a sulphate (50%). Such a result would be in keeping with a bituminous origin, the sulphate being produced by oxidation of sulphides present in fresh bitumen. Similar observations have been made on known bituminous material after only some fifty years (continuous) exposure to the atmosphere. No melting or softening was noted up to 500°C.

WOODEN BOWL (Fig. 19)

The oak bowl came from the Furnace site, and was found in the debris on the bellows area. Neither the rim nor the details of the base could be reconstructed. The vessel must be presumed to be of sixteenth-century date.

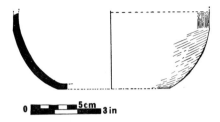

Fig. 19.   Wooden bowl: sixteenth century.   Scale: ¼

FURNACE BELLOWS PARTS (Fig. 20)

These objects of oak came from the bellows floor and are presumed to be parts of hinges mounted within the bellows, or, less likely, in some part of a lever system. As no parallels are known to exist for the period, this must be a conjectural identification. Object 6 in Fig. 20 was the most complete, a pair of jaws once fixed together by a thin iron strip, with some form of hinge joint at their head. 1–5, though fragmentary, were clearly similar, and 1, 2, and 5 bore holes which suggested that leather had been nailed to them. Agricola's illustrations do not help identification: he depicts (p. 365) hinges of a simpler kind.

THE ANIMAL BONES

By Dr Graeme Barker

A small sample of animal bones was recovered from the Chingley excavations, With one exception the bones were found in Period I levels at the forge; the exception was a shaft fragment of a cattle humerus found at the blast furnace. Of the 61 fragments from the forge, all those identifiable are of domestic animals. Table I lists the identifiable fragments, showing the numbers and percentages of the various species represented.

TABLE I   Numbers and percentages of identifiable fragments

	number of fragments	percentage of identifiable bones
horse	5	12
cattle	21	51
sheep/goat	6	15
pig	6	15
bird (chicken-size)	3	7
unidentifiable	20	—
TOTAL	61	100

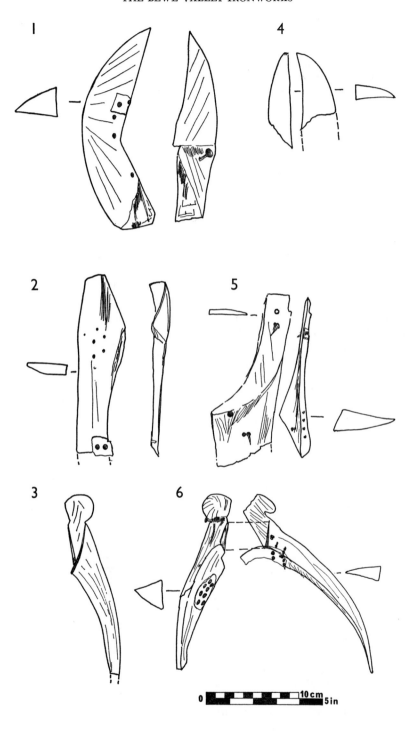

Fig. 20.   Bellows parts: Furnace.   Scale: ¼

Because the sample is so small, it is extremely difficult to calculate with any confidence the minimum number of individuals. Table II is at least a guide to this figure, showing the numbers of fragments found of the principal anatomical elements represented in the sample.

TABLE II Minimum numbers of individuals

	mandible	teeth	scapula	humerus	radius	ulna	pelvis	femur	tibia	meta-podials	TOTAL
horse	–	4	–	–	–	–	–	–	–	–	4
cattle	1	2	5	1	2	2	–	1	1	1	16
sheep/goat	–	1	–	–	–	–	1	3	1	–	6
pig	–	–	–	1	1	–	–	–	1	2	5

It must be emphasized that any interpretation of these figures is almost impossible for so small a sample. However, at least the importance of cattle is apparent in both tables and this dominance is probably all the more significant in view of the fact that cattle yield more than twice as much meat per animal as sheep, goats or swine. Butchering marks were not detected in the sample, but the overall fragmentation suggests that most of the fragments are the domestic refuse of meals taken by the occupants of the site. The lack of any bias in Table II towards a particular part or joint of the animal might perhaps imply that the cattle were butchered nearby.

Tables III and IV below list the mortality and metric data respectively taken from the Chingley forge samples.

TABLE III Mortality data (after Silver)

	long bone fusion (in months)	tooth eruption (in months)
cattle	+12/18 ... 1 −24/30 ... 1	+5/6 1
pig	+12 ..... 1 −24 ..... 1 −27 1	
sheep/goat		+3/5 1

SILVER, I. A. (1969), 'The ageing of domestic animals', in BROTHWELL, D., and HIGGS, E. S., *Science in Archaeology* (London, 1969), pp. 283–302.

TABLE IV Metric data taken from the Chingley sample (in millimetres)

cattle	metatarsal,	maximum width proximal epiphysis	32.1
		maximum thickness proximal epiphysis	31.8
pig	humerus,	maximum height distal articulation	16.0

MOLLUSCA

By Dr O. Lusis

8h (Period I)   Fresh-water mussel. Perhaps more likely, from its size, to be a pond mussel, but the shell is insufficiently complete to be certain that it is not a river mussel.

8b (Period II)   Oyster

ANIMAL FIBRES

By Professor F. J. G. Ebling
AND
Mr J. Skinner

Brush (Period I), Fig. 28:9

   This consisted of very dirty, stiff, stout fibres which were clearly animal hairs. The presence of a wide medulla suggests that they were from Horse (*Equus caballas*) and *not* Hog (*Sus scrofa*) bristles, which have a very fine medulla.

Wheel-pit (Period IIIB), Fig. 14

   The fibres were clearly animal hairs. They could be divided into two discrete categories: coarse hairs of diameters ranging from 70–125 µm, with either an unbroken medulla or an interrupted medulla of medium width, and fine hairs of 25–50 µm width without any medulla. It is most probable that these are hairs of the Domestic Ox (*Bos taurus*). They compared closely in range of diameters and medullary characteristics with hairs taken from the winter coat of a modern cow. In contrast, body hair from a Horse (*Equus caballas*) could not be easily sub-divided, they ranged from 40–110 µm in diameter and had a characteristic unbroken wide lattice medulla.

Chafery Wheel Jointing (Period IIIB), Fig. 9a:3

   These fibres were clearly animal hairs. They ranged in diameter from about 25–70 µm, and all appeared to have some medulla, either unbroken of medium width or interrupted. The absence of any stout fibres with continuous wide lattice medulla makes it unlikely they are Horse. They do not fit the pattern of the adult Ox, but it is probable, though not certain, that they are from a calf of *Bos taurus*.

MEDIEVAL POTTERY

This material can be divided into three groups: 1. The glazed wares; 2. Unglazed oxidized wares with light pink surfaces and fabrics; 3. Unglazed reduced grey and black wares.

1.   Glazed sherds were found in the filling of the re-cut foundation trench for the Period I race, associated with the replacement of the sideboards on the eastern side (**9H**), in the bottom silt of the race (**9E**), and scattered in the working debris to the east of the race (**8H**).

Fig. 21:15.   **9E.** Body sherd of Rye ware jug, in smooth grey oxidized fabric, unglazed inside with dark-speckled mid-green glaze. Two 'raspberry' stamp impressions on clay pressed out from within.[1]

---

[1] S. E. Rigold, 'Two Kentish Hospitals re-examined', *Archaeologia Cantiana*, 79 (1964), fig. 11:7, *c*. 1300.

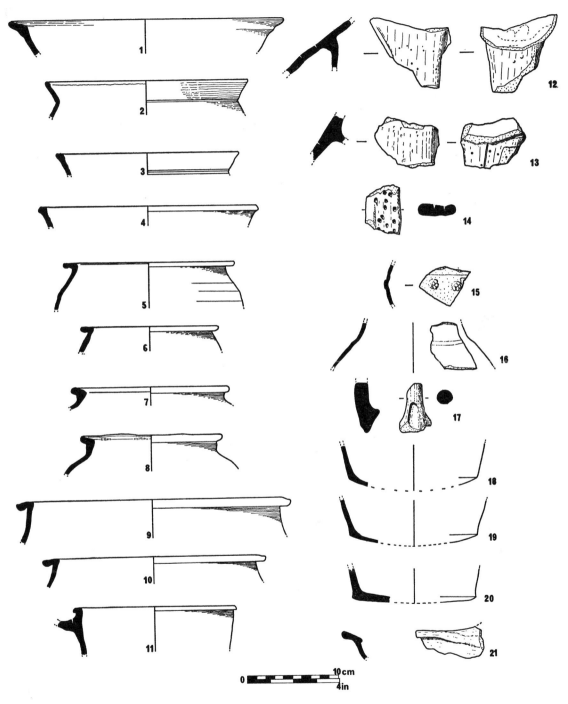

Fig. 21. Medieval Pottery. Scale: $\frac{1}{4}$

21:17. **8H.** Lower handle root from small jug: in buff fabric with splash of thin dull light green glaze. One thumb impression.

21:16. **9H.** Sherd from shoulder and neck of jug in dull orange fabric with sandy unglazed interior. Outside glazed dark khaki brown with excellent shiny surface apart from a rough patch on the neck. Traces of a splash of white slip beneath the glaze showing at the break, although the surface appearance of the glaze over the splash is a dull dark grey, almost black.

n.i. **9E.** Three small body sherds in dull grey fabric (A) with a varying slight tendency to pink. The inner surfaces are unglazed, and appear slightly pink, although one is encrusted with soot. The outer glaze is an uneven dark khaki.

9E. Six small body sherds in hard red fabric with an unglazed slightly pink inner surface similar to the others from **9E** (above). The uneven khaki glaze is also apparent, but on three of the sherds white slip has been applied before glazing. This shows as a more distinct light splash than on the sherd from **9H** (above).

8H. Nine small body sherds, probably from the same vessel, similar to (A) (above), but with a pinker fabric.

8H. One body sherd generally similar to (A) but perhaps from a thicker-walled vessel.

8H. One body sherd in sandy red fabric sandwiching a reduced purple core. Unglazed sandy buff-pink surface inside, dark brown outside with slight glaze dusting giving a tendency to purple.

N.B. *n.i.* = not illustrated.

UNGLAZED WARES

2. The oxidized fabrics.[1] This division is tentative and may be misleading. Layers **8H**, **9C**, and **9E** produced a few sherds pink to light grey in fabric and finish. Their numbers could be substantially reduced if, in the first place, some were fragments of vessels other parts of which were glazed; indeed the fabrics seen in category 1 were very similar. On the other hand, the grey wares, discussed below, covered a wide range of colour, and the division between the lightest greys and the pinky greys is not exact. Of the really distinct coarse sandy pink wares, there were only two fragments in **9E** and one in **8H**. The sagging base sherd illustrated from **8H** (Fig. 21, no. 18 from layer **8H**) though pink in fabric and surfaces was less sandy and could have come from a partly glazed jug. There was also one unusual body sherd in **8J**, with light smooth buff fabric and surfaces.

3. Reduced Grey Wares. This was by far the largest category; the material was prolific in the lower silt of the race (**9E**), the upper silt, around the wheel (**9C**), the working area (**8H**), the filling behind the replacement sideboards of the race (**9H** and **9J**), the slipped scatter sealing these infills (**8J**) and was residual on the site as late as the levelling undertaken for the Period II race (layers **8C** and **8D**), where it was found in the same deposits as sixteenth or early seventeenth-century material. The range of types of what has been called West Kent ware has been considered by Mr S. E. Rigold in his Eynsford Castle report.[2] The material from Chingley takes the distribution southwards, but goes no further to identify the source. Such products of the Limpsfield kilns as are accessible[3] are sufficiently similar in appearance to suggest a common intention, but, as with the Eynsford sherds, the Chingley material is different enough to have been made elsewhere. The rather open sandy grey surfaces at Limpsfield are not seen;

[1] For a discussion of the pinker East Weald wares see Rigold ibid., 61.
[2] See S. E. Rigold, 'Eynsford Castle and its Excavation', *Archaeologia Cantiana*, 85 (1971), 156 ff.
[3] I am grateful to Mr F. Holling for showing me the material in Guildford Museum.

rather there are fine-grain surfaces and the colour range includes many dark greys, and surfaces which could almost be called black-burnished. There were few cases of strongly shell-gritted ware. Certain of the New Romney material (Rigold 1964) shares these characteristics, as does that from the unpublished site at Leigh, ten miles north-west of Chingley. On balance the Chingley material comes closest to that found in Eynsford, Period D, ending in 1312.

The wares comprise cooking-pots, bowls, and jugs. Most of the cooking-pot rims have flat tops, with a bottom chamfer, although in some cases the out-turn has drooped somewhat (21:9); on occasion (21:6) there is a shallow groove running parallel to the edge on top of the rim. A small minority had simple upward flaring rims (21:2–3). Slight grooves (21:5) appear on the girths of certain vessels, some in groups of four to six, particularly on the lighter grey wares: while on others, particularly the blacker wares, there are wide bands of three faint parallel marks. Bases, of which relatively few were found, were sagging in all cases (21:18–20).

The bowls, of which few could be definitely identified, had rims similar to the cooking-pots (21:4), and one of these appeared to have had a pouring spout (21:21).

The jugs covered the same range of black and greys; their strap handles were thick, almost clumsy at the upper root, without thumbing, and some with small stab-marks on their upper and sometimes (21:13) lower surfaces. Some vessels presumed, from their smaller diameters, to be jugs rather than bowls or pots, had thumb-smoothing around their bases (21:19, 20). A representative sample is illustrated in Fig. 21 comprising about half the rims, half the bases, and all the handle fragments found. There were in addition a large quantity of small body sherds. In no case could a complete profile be built up.

Fig. 21: 1. **9E.** Bowl in fine sandy-grey fabric with sparse shell-gritting visible through pock-marks in the dark grey semi-burnished surface. Diameter 30 cm.

21: 2. **8H.** Flared rim of jar or cooking-pot. Slight shell gritting. The outside is smoke blackened, but the inner surface is one of the nearest approaches to the Limpsfield grey. Even so, it is not sufficiently sandy in surface texture. Diameter 22 cm.

21: 3, 4. **8H.** Less strongly-flared rims in a sandy grey fabric without grits. Heavily and presumably purposely black-surfaced inside and out. Diameters 20 cm.; 24 cm.

21: 5. **9E.** Fabric similar to 3 and 4 but tending to break up along laminations in the clay. The globular profile is repeated on several of the larger body sherds. Maximum surviving diameter at girth 21 cm.

21: 6. **9C.** A typical form, but a much more grey surface on a coarse sandy fabric. Diameter at rim, 17 cm.

21: 7. **9E.** A typically square-cut rim, but somewhat unusual in its angle. Close ungritted grey fabric with black surfaces. Diameter at rim, 17 cm.

21: 8. **8H.** A rather high-shouldered jar with an uneven rim; in places its top is horizontal. Slight shell gritting in rough grey fabric, visible through pock-marks in black surface inside and out. Maximum surviving girth diameter 19.5 cm.

21: 9, 10. **8C, 9E.** Distorted rims in fabrics and finishes similar to 8. Diameter of rims 30 cm.; 24.5 cm.

21:11. **8H.** Light sandy grey fabric and surfaces. Stab marks on outer surface of handle. Rim diameter about 18 cm.

21:12, 13. **9H, 9C.** Handle-roots in grey fabric, 13 rather the coarser, and with stab marks on the underside, in contrast to those on the top of the handle of 12. Black surfaces.

21:14. **9E.** Strap handle in rough grey fabric with grey surfaces. Some stabs on the upper surface have been done with vigour sufficient to cause pimpling on the underside.

21:15–17. See glazed wares, above.

21:18. See unglazed oxidized fabrics, above.

21:19. **8H.** Base-angle sherd of sagging-base jar or pot in buff-grey fabric with sparse shell-gritting. Diameter at base, 14 cm.

21:20. **9E.** A similar form but in an unusually black fabric. Diameter at base 14 cm.

21:21. **9H.** A form unique on the site: a rim from a bowl far more massive in its rim section than 21:1, and with traces of the edge of a pouring-spout. Diameter uncertain.

POST-MEDIEVAL POTTERY

The clearest deposits of sixteenth-century pottery came from the furnace. Apart from three small nineteenth-century sherds in the topsoil over the collapsed structure, all the material from this site corresponded with its known period of operation. The Frechen and Raeren stonewares, the manganese-glazed and unglazed jars and skillets, and the coarse earthenwares fit well into the middle and later years of the sixteenth century. The unusual piece of marbled earthenware reminiscent of Cistercian ware was of interest, but, probably being a style derived from rather than within the main line of Cistercian-ware development, cannot be used to take the dating of the furnace much further back than the first documentary information in 1565.

At the forge the sixteenth-century material was ill-defined. In layer **8D** there was a sherd similar to Fig. 23:1 from the furnace, deposited before or during the construction of the Period II race. The unglazed earthenware from **8G** probably comes from the period of use of II, when little pottery appears to have been deposited.

The extent of rebuilding and conversion on the site in the seventeenth century inevitably produces the risk of residual pottery finding its way into late contexts, and the long currency of local coarse wares over the period also hinders precision. In layer **5F**, the lower silt of the IIIA stone-lined race (Fig. 5d) was found a body sherd of a Type II Flemish stoneware flask of the sixteenth century, this came from low in the silt near where the finery wheel is presumed to have been mounted, and its presence is a problem. It is perhaps most likely to have been deposited late, with residual rubbish, even as late as the late seventeenth century, although it could have been dropped into the dam end of the race at a much earlier period and reached the finery wheel end after a long delay, particularly if silting had been allowed in the south end of the race after it had ceased to be used for a hammer-wheel (p. 24 above). Even so, activity on the site in the sixteenth century is suggested by its presence.

Apart from this, the coarse wares and stonewares present no problems, and are consistent with deposit through the seventeenth century and into the eighteenth. The first appearance of Fulham stoneware (made from 1671) comes in layer **7S**, the silt of the IIIB tailrace, confirming the use of the race around 1700. In the abandonment layers, typically **7G**, come late stonewares, a London (probably Bankside) mug (22:9) being useful.

(In the text below, sherds will be mentioned within their ware-categories, in approximate order of deposition.)

STONEWARES

Furnace

Fig. 23: 3. Layer **11**. Black material probably slipped from abutment of charging bridge. 2 sherds of Frechen jug.

23: 4. **6.** Silt over wheel-pit. Base of Frechen jug.

n.i. **2.** collapsed rubble over hearth. Shoulder of Frechen jug, with coarser mottling than the sherds in layer **11**.

Forge

    n.i. **5F.** bottom silt of eastern (stone) race. Body sherd of Flemish flask in grey stoneware, Type II. (See J. G. Hurst, note in E. J. E. Pirie, 'Kirkstall Abbey Excavations', *Thorsesby Soc.*, 51 (1967), 54–9.)

    n.i. **3A.** Cinder levelling for floor west of IIIв wheel-pit. Small body sherd, possibly English.

22: 2. **3A.** Polychrome body sherd. Westerwald, late seventeenth century.

    n.i. **7S.** Low silt in IIIв tailrace. Small body sherd, Frechen.

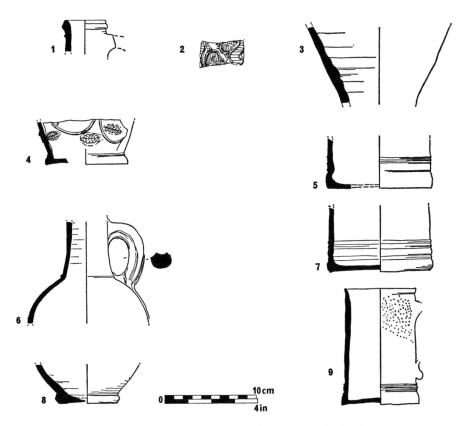

Fig. 22. Stonewares from the Forge. Scale: ¼

22: 3. **7S.** Body sherd. Fulham. After 1671.

22: 8. **4F.** Top cinder floor, around small re-working hearths, south of finery. Base: Frechen.

    n.i. **4F.** Body sherd. Frechen.

22: 5. **4F.** Base of mug. Frechen.

    n.i. **4F.** Body sherd. Frechen.

22: 4. **7K.** Chafery pit. Base, Cologne.

22: 9.   **7G.**   Silt and debris immediately over IIIB wheel-pit. Base, probably London (Bankside).[1]

n.i.   **7G.**   Two small body sherds. Frechen.

n.i.   **7G.**   Small body sherd, possibly Nottingham.

22: 1.   **3C.**   Neck and handle root of flagon/jug, but in very dark stoneware with splashes of khaki/green glaze.

22: 6.   **5A/3C.**   Top silt of E. race, demolition layer and subsequent topsoil. Joining sherds of handle and neck of Frechen jug.

22: 7.   **3C/1A.**   Joining sherds of base and wall of ?Bankside mug.

n.i.   **3C.**   Small body sherd ?Cologne.

n.i.   **1A.**   Frechen, 4 small body sherds, 1 handle fragment.

EARTHENWARES

Furnace

Fig. 23: 6.   Layer **33.**   Early silt in tailrace culvert. Body sherd of laminated dark purple and light grey fabric giving a marbled effect on the outer surface, through a clear glaze, and a purple surface inside. Slight horizontal marking on the inside, vertical ribbing on the outside. The purple part of the fabric is reminiscent of the partly self-glazing post-Cistercian-ware fabrics of the Midlands, but parallels are lacking for this interesting variant.

23: 1.   In $\begin{cases} \textbf{26.} & \text{Orange to blue-grey clay in tuyere arch; and} \\ \textbf{29.} & \text{Blacky leafy and mossy deposit under the bellows:} \end{cases}$ 17 sherds, several joining, of tripod-based skillet in red-purple-grey fabric, oxidized near outer surfaces, with reduced core; brown manganese-flecked glaze inside and splashed over outside. Zone of scored decoration around the shoulder.

23: 8.   In **26.**   Two joining body sherds in thick coarse dull red fabric. Apparently from a pitcher of about 23 cm. girth. Splashes of dark green glaze inside and out, with some self-glazing purple effect inside.

n.i.   In **34.**   Upper silt around wheel fragment; base in red fabric with similar glazing to 23:1 (above). Base diameter 10.2 cm.

n.i.   In **25.**   Black gritty layer, the uppermost working surface in the tuyere arch: 4 body sherds of vessel in dull red fabric with manganese glaze over upper part; perhaps belonging to 23:1.

1 body sherd of globular vessel, about 21.5 cm. diameter at the girth, unglazed outside, crazed khaki inside.

1 body sherd of unglazed dull red ware.

In **6.**   Silt and rubble over the wheel-pit:

n.i.   2 sherds (1 base angle, 12.7 cm. diameter) in pale red clay with pink-washed surfaces.

23: 7.   Handle root in rough light red fabric with splash of light orange glaze on thumb impression.

23: 2.   Jar in dark grey reduced slightly gritted fabric with unglazed red surfaces.

23: 5.   Base sherd in smoother fabric than 23:2, but from apparently similar vessel.

n.i.   In **22.**   Spread of rubble from SW. buttress of furnace: body sherd with fine light pink fabric and interior surface, smoke blackened outside. Diameter of girth approximately 28 cm.

---

[1] A. H. Oswald, 'A London Stoneware Pottery' *Connoisseur*, 126 (January 1951), 183. I am grateful to Mr J. H. Ashdown for this reference.

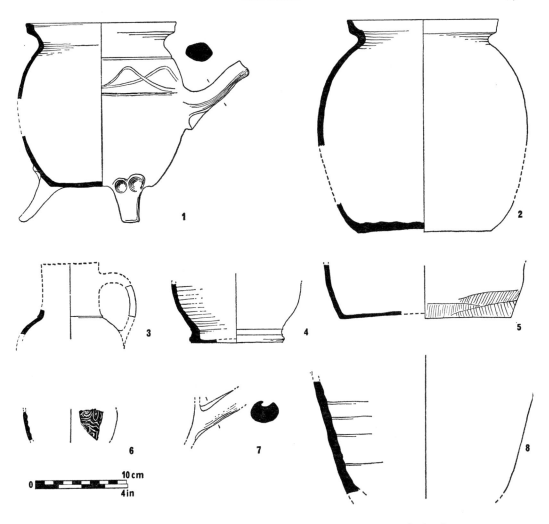

Fig. 23. Sixteenth-century pottery from the Furnace. Scale: ¼

n.i. In **2**. Upper rubble: small rim and body fragments of vessel similar to 23:2 but with splash of very dark khaki glaze on rim. Rim 20.3 cm. diameter.

n.i. In **2**. Base of small jug in light orange fabric with light brown glaze inside, and splashed on outside. Diameter of footring 7.7 cm.

The Forge

n.i. In **8D**. Blue-grey clay, perhaps the final silt before the Period II race was built, or a levelling-up deposit for it: 1 small body sherd of sixteenth-century dull red fabric with interior manganese glaze.

n.i. In **8G**. A similar deposit, immediately north of the end of the Period II timbers, and hard to relate to them: 2 unglazed sherds of bright and relatively fine fabric with blackened outside and brown inside surfaces. Probably from a large jar.

n.i.   In **8D.**   Period II wheel-pits, particularly on west side (Fig. 5a): 3 sherds forming most of base of jug or jar in sandy fabric varying from buff to dark grey. Small splash of purple/black glaze on footring. 12 cm. diameter at base.

All three of these would fit reasonably but not exclusively in a mid sixteenth-century deposit.

n.i.   In **7R.**   Build-up for Period IIIB, over the Period II wheel-pit (Fig. 5a): two sherds from the girth of a large jar at least 25.4 cm. diameter, in bright red fabric with a brown/purple wash inside and outside.

Fig. 24: 3.   In **4N.**   Cinder and charcoal: 4 rim fragments of jar or jug in dull pink-orange fabric with bright brown glaze inside, and splashed on outside. Also sherd from a base, not illustrated, perhaps from the same or similar vessel.

24: 1.   **4B.**   Patches of hard cinder associated with the reheating hearths north of the finery (Fig. 14) and little different from the cinder and charcoal **4N** (Fig. 5a) and **5F**, lower silt of IIIA race — southern length: a large number of sherds from the seventeenth-century pitcher illustrated, showing that silt had built up to a

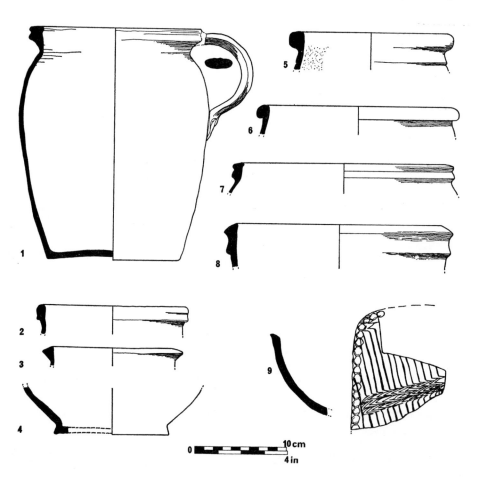

Fig. 24.   Post-medieval coarsewares from the Forge.   Scale: ¼

depth of 53 cm. in the stone-lined race when **4B** was still being laid down during the use of the reheating hearths.

n.i.   In **4H.**   Hard cinder surface between the finery bellows area and the chafery: body sherd of pink fabric with rough manganese glaze, probably from a small sixteenth-century jug or cup.

n.i.   In **4F.**   Hard working-surface round edge of pit in finery building: body sherd in orange fabric with much rust-blackened brown/manganese glaze. Probably from between rim and handle-root of small jug. Probably early seventeenth century.

3A.   Cinder levelling for floor west of IIIB wheel-pit.

24: 5.   Rim in dull pink fabric, unglazed outside, dark red-brown glaze inside.

: 8.   Rim in brighter pink fabric, with pink wash outside and bright brown glaze inside. In addition, a number of rim, base and body fragments of similar seventeenth-century wares.

n.i.   Handle sherd in grey fabric with purple glaze. More a sixteenth-century type.

7S.   Lower silt in IIIB tailrace.

n.i.   2 body sherds of thirteenth/fourteenth-century black ware (see p. 48 above), presumably resulting from disturbance of the early levels during construction of IIIB. See depressions marked (III) in Fig. 6.

24: 7.   Rim sherd in grey fabric, unglazed but with slight pink wash. Base and body fragments (not illustrated) could have belonged to this vessel.

n.i.   Two small abraded rim fragments of white majolica bowl, probably Netherlands Delft, mid-late seventeenth century.

4A.   Demolition debris: charcoal stained soil and rubble over the forge:

24: 4.   Base and body sherds of bowl or perhaps jug in bright orange fabric with thick shiny brown glaze.

7G.   Silt and debris in and immediately over IIIB wheel-pit.

24: 2.   Rim in very dark grey fabric with dull brown glaze.

24: 9.   Staffordshire rectangular platter in buff fabric with yellow slip feathered through to brown slip.

n.i.   Thumbed jug-handle root in red fabric with purple-brown internal glaze. Probably a residual sixteenth-century piece. Also a base fragment in similar ware. The topsoil deposits, **3C** and **1A**, contained material duplicating the above, and included a further rim, in red fabric with internal brown glaze (Fig. 24:6).

DECORATED ROOF TILE

Fragments of a decorated tile **8H** were reconstructed as in Fig. 25. These have been examined by Mr G. C. Dunning and Mr K. J. Barton, and while no exact parallels are known, they both suggest some form of decorated roof tile in the Rye tradition. The exact type is in doubt, but it is suggested (K.J.B.) that the bellying-out of the angle of the tile might indicate a fragment of some kind of raised decorative ridge-piece.

The key elements in the decoration indicating an East Sussex or West Kent origin are: the white coating, with trefoils in black or green glaze, a Rye tradition; the jabbing technique on the top angle, a technique seen in West Kent–East Sussex pottery in general; the angular rather than rounded form, suggesting an East rather than West Sussex style of tile.

The dating may be later rather than earlier in the fourteenth century, as these scroll patterns seem to come relatively late on Rye pottery. This view of the date (K.J.B.) does not conflict

E

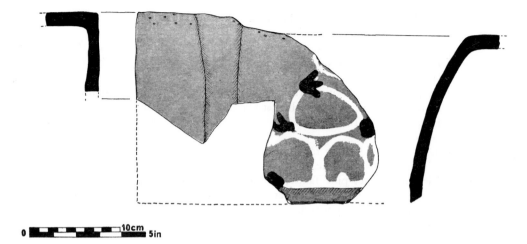

Fig. 25.   Medieval roof-tile.   Scale: $\frac{1}{4}$

with the other ceramic evidence; for although the latter tends to put the site earlier in the fourteenth century, the types of pottery could have survived in use up to the Black Death period, and the tile, perhaps part of a repair or rebuild of the roof, could belong to the middle decades, soon after the documentary references.

CLAY TOBACCO PIPES

By D. R. ATKINSON

The material from Chingley Forge contains only a small range of types, and the date range, apart from some Victorian pieces from the topsoil, is about thirty years, *c.* 1690–1720, plus or minus ten years each way. The only maker identifiable with certainty is Thomas Harman of Lewes. The other initials, H/I, S/P, M/H and E/M probably represent local Kent makers, as they are not isolated examples on this site. All the pipes are of the contemporary London style, which was copied in Kent and Sussex. The group is typical of the William III–Anne-George I period in south-eastern England, and contains nothing unusual or requiring illustration.

CATALOGUE (the A&O numbers refer to the Atkinson and Oswald London typology)[1]
Layer

1A   topsoil   Bowl *c.* 1690, A&O 18–20.
                                       Bowl *c.* 1720, A&O 25. Initials H/I (unknown).
                                       1 piece, *c.* 1700–20. Initials S/P (unknown).
                                       1 piece, *c.* 1700–20. Large initials, indistinct.
                                       Several nineteenth-century pieces. One spur (*c.* 1850) has initials T/S (unknown).

---

[1] D. R. Atkinson and A. H. Oswald, 'London Clay Tobacco Pipes', *Journal of the British Archaeological Association*, 32 (1969), 171–227.

3A	spread of cinder	1 piece *c.* 1720, A&O 25. Initials H/I.
3B	from flattened dam	1 piece *c.* 1700–20, A&O 25 (early). Initials S/P.
3C	(Section A–B)	Several plain pieces, late seventeenth/early eighteenth century.
		1 piece unmarked, *c.* 1700–20.
		1 piece *c.* 1690–1700, A&O 20 or 22. Initials R/H (unknown).
		1 piece *c.* 1720–40, A&O 25. Initials H/I.
4B	Top cinder working debris on forge floor (A–B)	Pipe, *c.* 1690–1700, London type, A&O 21. Unmarked.
		1 piece with crowned but illegible initials, *c.* 1720–40, A&O 25.
4F	Mixed clay and hard cinder: finery floor (G–H and N–O)	2 pieces, one with spur, *c.* 1690.
4N	Forge floor — cinder (N–O)	1 piece, eighteenth century.
		Bowl, *c.* 1690, A&O 15–19.
	Fulcrum pit on top filling (A–B)	Bowl, *c.* 1690–1700, A&O 20–2. Unmarked.
	post-holes 13	1 piece, *c.* 1700.
	14	Bowl, *c.* 1690–1700, A&O 18–22. Unmarked.
5A	Upper silt of finery channel (A–B)	Bowl, *c.* 1690, A&O 20.
		Bowl, *c.* 1700–20, A&O 25 (early). Initials R/H (?).
		3 pieces, *c.* 1690–1720.
5F	Lower silt of finery channel (A–B)	Bowls and fragments, all late seventeenth/early eighteenth-century, London types A&O 20–2. All unmarked.
7A	Hammer and block wood chips below cinder 4N (A–B)	Bowl, late seventeenth-century. Type uncertain.
	Anvil pit: top of filling (A–B)	1 piece, *c.* 1720–40, A&O 25. Initials M/H (unknown).
7B	Around and under smithing hearths in forge	Pipe, *c.* 1680–90, A&O 18–20. Unmarked.
		1 piece, *c.* 1690–1700. Unmarked.
7G	Destruction layer in and over breast wheel-pit (A–B, C–D)	2 bowls, *c.* 1690, A&O 18–20. Unmarked.
		1 bowl, *c.* 1720, A&O 25. Initials E/M (unknown).
		1 bowl, *c.* 1700–20, A&O 25 (early). Unmarked.
		Pipe, *c.* 1720–30, London type A&O 25. Moulded initials T/H: Thomas Harman of Lewes, 1697–1781.
		Another by the same maker, but perhaps *c.* 1720–40.
		1 bowl, *c.* 1720–40, A&O 25. Unmarked.
		1 piece, similar type and dating. Initials H/I.
		1 piece of eighteenth-century bowl, probably *c.* 1720.
7N	Demolition deposit, contemp. with 7G.	1 piece, *c.* 1720, A&O 25. Initials H/I.
7Q	hard cinder floor around hand anvil Pd. III (A–B)	1 piece, *c.* 1690. Unmarked.

7S	Hammer and Chafery tailrace silt (C–D)	Bowl, *c.* 1720, A&O 25. 2 pipes, *c.* 1720–40, A&O 25. Initials E/M. 1 bowl, similar.

8B
8C { Deposits over period
2 wheel-pit, alongside
Pd. III hammer-race

2 pipes, *c.* 1720–40, A&O 25. 1 plain, 1 with initials T/C (unknown)

2 bowls, *c.* 1720, A&O. 25 Initials E/M and S/P (unknown makers).

(The presence of these late fragments is not a conclusive argument for eighteenth-century construction of the Period III hammer and chafery race, for the pieces came from the north ends of these layers, where they were not sealed by 3Q.)

THE GLASS

Fragments of two objects came from deposits of Period IIIB.

Fig. 26, 1.   Layer 5a. Base of small bowl in colourless glass; early eighteenth century.
    26, 2.   Layer 7G. Neck of bottle in green glass; early eighteenth century.

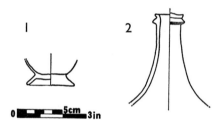

Fig. 26.   Glass.   Scale: $\frac{1}{4}$

METAL OBJECTS

DEPOSITS OF SCRAP AND UNIDENTIFIABLE MATERIAL

In Period III deposits at the forge, quantities of iron were found which can only be described as scrap. In layer **7S** there were numerous pieces of flat plate and strip which showed signs of having been cut or chipped. Many had been used, as indicated by holes and lengths of straight edge. It must be assumed that in the course of fabrication of the forge's products iron derived from objects either brought in or rejected in manufacture had been cut up to make components such as washers.

BLOOM

By DR R. F. TYLECOTE

From the wheel-pit at the furnace. This is clearly a bloom of wrought iron. Slag fibres show clearly that it is typical bloomery iron, heterogeneous and not unlike the Newcastle experimental bloom no. 21.[1] The hardness readings of the Chingley worked bloom, or billet, were as

---

[1] R. F. Tylecote, J. N. Austin, and A. E. Wraith, 'The Mechanism of the Bloomery Process in Shaft Furnaces', *Journal of the Iron and Steel Institute*, 209 (1971), 342–63.

follows: 92, 111, 118 HV10. Its presence in the furnace wheel-pit is odd, but must suggest earlier working near by.

This is a very valuable object since it must be almost unique. The nearest that I know of is a bar or gad (from Winchester) which comes from a somewhat earlier period. That object, however, only measures 2 × ⅜ in. section and about 1 ft long; it is also a piece of bloomery iron, and not steel.

Bloom of Refined Iron from the Forge (Period III)
By Dr R. F. Tylecote

Layer 7S.   This consists of low-carbon iron immersed in slag and could well be a piece of a bloom or oxidized metal from the finery. However, it has not been forged, and the ferrite areas which have a hardness of 120 HV5 appear to have no carbon gradient as might have been expected if the material had come from a finery.

One of the more interesting features is the presence of pieces of 'fossil' charcoal in the slag surrounding the ferrite areas. The charcoal has for the most part disappeared and been replaced by a slag replica. These are replicas of pieces of wood or charcoal in longitudinal and cross section and it would seem that the wood was diffuse-porous rather than the ring-porous oak which one usually finds on iron smelting sites in this country. It is just possible that these are replicas of the more slow growing autumn and winter wood of oak, but I doubt it. I have seen this effect once before — on hammer scale from Stoney Hazel in Furness. How it is produced is rather a problem since it cannot be the result of the fluid slag filling the pores in the charcoal since these are still empty, and the slag appears to have replaced the vessel walls. I can only put forward the suggestion that the fluidity of the slag has been lowered by the fluxing action of the ash content of the vessel walls and the slag has been kept out of the pores by gas pressure. Obviously this effect wants a lot more investigation.

The fact that the wood is diffuse-porous and probably beech is one point in support of the possibility that this metal is from the finery and not the bloomery. According to Vandermonde, Berthollet and Monge,[1] in 1786, soft woods such as beech, which could not be used in the blast furnace because of their low mechanical strength, were used in the finery where, in addition, their greater reactivity was an advantage. It must be remembered also that the furnace at Stoney Hazel appears to have been a finery hearth.[2] Of course, the softer woods could have been used in the bloomery; but this was certainly not normal practice in the north of England.

Conclusion   This is a piece from a bloom that has been made from a low-phosphorus ore with a diffuse-porous wood such as beech. It has a low carbon content (less than 0.1%) and has not been forged.

CHINGLEY FORGE METALWORK
By Ian H. Goodall
with contributions by H. L. Blackmore, Alan Borg, and Blanche Ellis

Objects which have been X-rayed are marked*. Items marked † are the subject of a metallurgical report, below, pp. 90–107.

---

[1] C. S. Smith (ed.) *Sources for the History of the Science of Steel (1532–1786)* (Cambridge, Massachusetts, 1968), p. 334.

[2] M. Davies-Shiel, 'Excavations at Stoney Hazel, High Furness . . .'. *Bulletin of the Historical Metallurgy Group*, 4/1 (1970), 28–32.

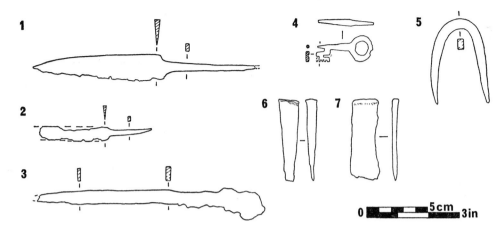

Fig. 27.   Chingley Forge. Iron objects. Period I.   Scale: $\frac{1}{3}$

IRON OBJECTS: Period I (Fig. 27)

†1.   Knife with incomplete whittle tang. **9E**
†2.   Knife with whittle tang and incomplete blade. **9E.**
3.   Knife mood or blank, tang corroded. **9H.**
†4.   Key with ring bow, tapering stem and incomplete toothed bit. **9E.**
5.   U-shaped staple. **9C.**
6–7.   Small wedges, each weighing 1½ oz. (43 gm.), 6:**9E**, 7:**9H**.
       Nails: see section at end of Chingley Furnace metalwork report.

COPPER ALLOY OBJECTS: Period I (Fig. 28)

†1, †2.   Strap-end buckles with forked attachments, 1 complete with pin and riveted side-plates. Similar examples include those from London and Riseholme, Lincolnshire.[1] **9E.**
3.   Sheet metal buckle pin, loop flattened. **9E.**
†4.   One plate of a belt chape with two rivets in place. Compare with examples from Seacourt, Oxfordshire (Berkshire).[2] **9E.**
5.   Pin with double-twist head. **9E.**
†5a.   Pin with brass head. **9E.**   *Not illustrated.*
6.   Ring, circular section. **9E.**
†7.   Vessel leg. **9E.**
†8.   Fragment of gently curved object, 1.5 mm. thick. **9E.**   *Not illustrated.*

Small offcuts from strips of copper-base alloy, found in association with these objects (1–8) are discussed in the metallurgical report below.

LEAD ALLOY OBJECTS: Period I (Fig. 28)

9.   Tube, formed by bending round and roughly overlapping a lead sheet, enclosing horse hairs. Perhaps a brush. **9E.**

---

[1] *London Museum Medieval Catalogue* (London, 1967 edition), p. 272, pl. LXXV.1, 2; F. H. Thompson, 'The Deserted Medieval Village of Riseholme, near Lincoln', *Medieval Archaeology*, 4 (1960), 106, fig. 34.1.
[2] M. Biddle, 'The Deserted Medieval Village of Seacourt, Berkshire', *Oxoniensia*, 26–7 (1961–2), 168, fig. 28 4, 5.

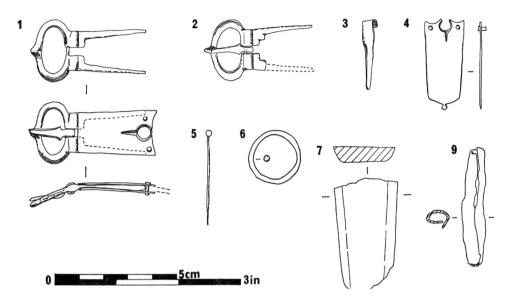

Fig. 28. Chingley Forge. Copper alloy (1–7) and lead (9) objects. Period I.
Scale: $\frac{2}{3}$

10. Tube 35 mm. long, 9 mm. diameter, distorted. **9E.** *Not illustrated.*

11–13. Three formerly rectangular fragments of lead sheet with nailholes. Larger pieces of roof leading are known from St Catharine's Hill, Winchester, Hampshire.[1] Maximum dimensions 28 × 30, 15 × 32, and 20 × 35 mm. respectively. **9E.** *Not illustrated.*

14. Scrap. Distorted rectangle 19 × 21 mm. **8H.** *Not illustrated.*

IRON OBJECTS: Periods II and III

KNIVES (Fig. 29)

Knives with whittle and scale tangs are known from medieval and later contexts, but the bolster between blade and tang found on 2, 3, and 4 is a sixteenth-century introduction. The bolster, made from a single piece of iron, represents an advance in technique since it replaces the applied shoulder plates of medieval knives. Hayward[2] suggests that this change in the method of hafting knives took place about the middle of the sixteenth century or a little later, although apparently earlier examples include that from a 1540 Dissolution destruction level (F.64) in Building I at Waltham Abbey, Essex.[3] The different forms of bolster reflect something of the variety found amongst post-medieval knives. 2 and 3 are similar to those of knives from Basing House, Hampshire,[4] occupied 1531–1645.

[1] C. F. C. Hawkes, J. N. L. Myres, and C. E. Stevens, 'St. Catharine's Hill, Winchester', *Proc. Hampshire Field Club and Archaeological Society*, 11 (1930), 226, fig. 24.K.
[2] J. F. Hayward, *English Cutlery* (London, 1957), p. 4.
[3] P. J. Huggins, 'Monastic Grange and Outer Close Excavations, Waltham Abbey, Essex, 1970–1972', *Trans. Essex Archaeological Society*, 4 (1972), 41, 124.
[4] Stephen Moorhouse and Ian H. Goodall in Stephen Moorhouse, 'Finds from Basing House, Hampshire (c. 1540–1645): Part Two', *Post-Medieval Archaeology*, 5 (1971), 36–8, fig. 17.4, 10.

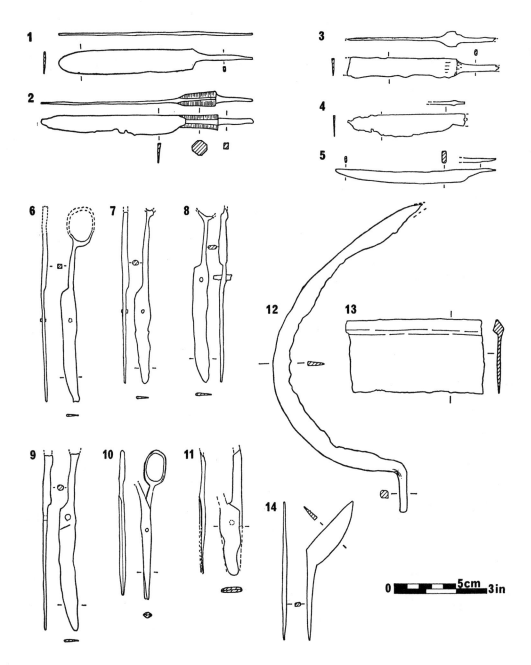

Fig. 29. Chingley Forge. Iron: knives, scissors, sickle, scythe and blade. Periods II–III. Scale: $\frac{1}{3}$

†1.   Knife, whittle tang, blade with rounded tip. **7S.**
†2.   Knife with broken whittle tang, long octagonal bolster and incomplete blade. **7S.**
  3.   Knife, whittle tang, short circular-section bolster, broken blade. **7S.**
  4.   Knife, base of scale tang, narrow bolster and incomplete blade. **7S.**
†5.   Knife mood or blank. **7S.**

Five strips, possibly moods or blanks, were also found in Layer **7S**, and are discussed in the metallurgical report below. *Not illustrated.*

Scissors, Sickle, Scythe, Blade (Fig. 29)

†6–11.   Scissor blades and incomplete pairs of scissors. **7S.**
   12.   Narrow-blade sickle, incomplete. **4N.**
†13.   Fragment of scythe blade with marked back-rib. **7G.**
†14.   Tanged blade, possibly a pruning knife. **7S.**

Wedges and Chisels (Fig. 30)

Of the total of thirty-two wedges and chisels, thirteen (15, 16, 30, 34, 36, 38, 40–6) are complete, four (32, 35, 37, 39) are complete but distorted, three (24, 26, 33) are worn, and twelve (17–23, 25, 27, 29, 31) are incomplete. 34, 42, 43, 45, and 46 are chisels, but it is impossible to be certain whether 26, 27, 32, 35–8 were used as chisels or small wedges. The remainder are wedges, the majority large. Several have burred heads, some the result of very heavy hammering, and they may have been used in quarrying. 33, as well as 30 and certain other broad but thin wedges, might have been used as slats: cf. 59 below. However, since metallurgical examination of five wedges showed them to be wrought iron, and to lack the steel edges which a tool would require, it is impossible not to suggest that many of the wedges served structural functions. Similar structural wedges are to be seen in the two hammers at Wortley Forge, South Yorkshire (West Riding, Yorkshire), SK 294999. Although both hammers have clearly been subject to extensive repair, the north hammer essentially retains an early eighteenth-century appearance, incorporating numerous wedges in its construction. It may nevertheless be noted that it was common medieval practice to weld a piece of steel on to the edge of cutting tools,[1] and this might explain the absence of steel on at least some of the Chingley Forge tools.

Table of Wedges and Chisels.

Dimensions taken below the head avoid any distortion caused by burring; those at the base are taken above any break. Measurements were taken before treatment, but allow for serious corrosion.

No.	Length	Dimensions below head	Dimensions at base (width if complete)	Description	Weight gm.	lb.	oz.	Context
15	247 mm.	85 × 23 mm.	87 mm.	Complete; *not illustrated.*	2137	4	11¼	**4N**
16	215 mm.	82 × 18 mm.	55 mm.	Complete; *not illustrated.*	1025	3	2	**8B**
17	196 mm.	66 × 25 mm.	50 mm.	Burred head, blade slightly damaged; *not illustrated.*	1368	3	0	**7N**
18	185 mm.	66 × 19 mm.	61 mm.	Heavily burred head, blade damaged.	1197	2	10	**7S**

---

[1] L. F. Salzman, *Building in England down to 1540. A documentary history* (Oxford, 1967 edition), pp. 330–1.

No.	Length	Dimensions below head	Dimensions at base (width if complete)	Description	Weight gm.	lb. oz.	Context
19	182 mm.	62×28 mm.	57 mm.	Burred head, blade damaged; *not illustrated.*	1168	2 9	**7P**
20	172 mm.	54×23 mm.	51 mm.	Burred head, blade damaged.	1026	2 4¾	**8C**
†21	190 mm.	62×12 mm.	55 mm.	Slightly burred head, blade slightly damaged; *not illustrated.*	827	1 13	**7G**
22	134 mm.	46×19 mm.	36×9 mm.	Head burred, base lost; *not illustrated.*	413	14½	**4N**
23	193 mm.	45×10 mm.	33 mm.	Head burred, blade damaged and distorted.	541	1 3	**7G**
24	145 mm.	54×13 mm.	42 mm.	Slightly burred head, blade worn; *not illustrated.*	570	1 4	**7G**
25	162 mm.	42×20 mm.	27×7 mm.	Base lost, shaft bent near break; *not illustrated.*	454	1 0	**4F**
†26	142 mm.	32×19 mm.	27 mm.	Head partly cut away, blade corner worn; *not illustrated.*	442	15½	**7G**
27	89 mm.	32×13 mm.	25×5 mm.	Base lost; *not illustrated.*	228	8	**7G**
28	129 mm.	62×11 mm.	61 mm.	Head burred, blade damaged and distorted.	371	13	**4N**
29	118 mm.	59×13 mm.	59 mm.	Head burred, corner of blade lost; *not illustrated.*	420	14¾	**7G**
30	110 mm.	58×11 mm.	59 mm.	Complete; *not illustrated.*	470	1 0½	**7G**
31	84 mm.	65× 8 mm.	54×5 mm.	Head burred, base lost; *not illustrated*	242	8½	**7G**
32	134 mm.	25×19 mm.	15 mm.	Slightly curved in side view; *not illustrated.*	242	8½	**5A**
33	137 mm.	31×10 mm.	15 mm.	Complete, blade edge rounded; *not illustrated.*	185	6½	**8B**
34	133 mm.	19×16 mm.	7 mm.	Complete, stem rounded at top but becoming rectangular.	156	5½	**7S**
35	114 mm.	20×20 mm.	8 mm.	Complete, slightly curved in side view; *not illustrated.*	163	5¾	**8C**
36	115 mm.	21×18 mm.	9 mm.	Complete, head slightly burred; *not illustrated.*	185	6½	**7G**
37	105 mm.	19×12 mm.	7 mm.	Complete but distorted; *not illustrated.*	64	2¼	**7X**
38	98 mm.	22×20 mm.	10 mm.	Complete head burred.	149	5¼	**7S**
39	100 mm.	16×10 mm.	10 mm.	Complete, slightly curved in side view; *not illustrated.*	71	2½	**7A**
40	88 mm.	21×11 mm.	7 mm.	Complete; *not illustrated.*	78	2¾	**8C**
†41	78 mm.	24×11 mm.	13 mm.	Complete.	86	3	**8C**
42	190 mm.	30×26 mm.	16 mm.	Complete, head burred.	555	1 3½	**5F**
†43	143 mm.	30×18 mm.	16 mm.	Complete, head burred.	413	14½	**7R**
44	125 mm.	23×14 mm.	16 mm.	Complete, head slightly burred.	213	7½	**7G**
45	165 mm.	25×22 mm.	9 mm.	Complete, head slightly burred.	428	15	**8C**
†46	99 mm.	14×14 mm.	9 mm.	Complete, head slightly burred.	100	3½	**7R**

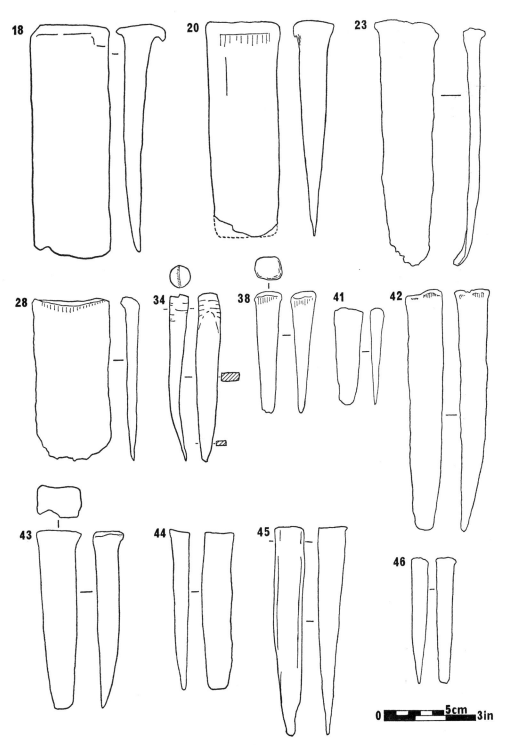

Fig. 30.   Chingley Forge. Iron: wedges and chisels. Periods II–III.   Scale: $\frac{1}{3}$

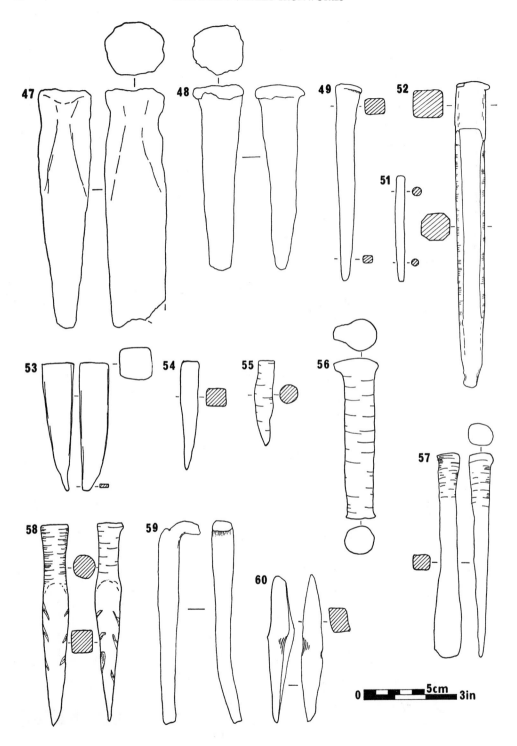

Fig. 31.   Chingley Forge. Iron: punches, drifts and stonemasons' tools. Periods II–III.
Scale: ⅓

PUNCHES AND DRIFTS (Fig. 31)

In metalworking, the punch was used to make a hole which was then opened out or enlarged with a drift of appropriate cross-section. The Chingley Forge punches and drifts vary considerably in size and shape. 47, with its shaped end, has a waisted body around which a handle fitted. 48 might be a quarrying plug rather than a punch: compare 59 below. 50 (*not illustrated*) is a punch 109 mm. long, 19 × 14 mm. below the slightly burred head, and 4 mm. square at its base.

Metallurgical examination of 54 showed that it would have been suitable for making holes for the rivets in scissors.

Weights and contexts: 47: 3 lb. 8 oz. (1596 gm.), **7G**; 48: 1 lb. 2½ oz. (527 gm.), **7R**; 49: 5 oz. (143 gm.), **8B**; 50: 2¾ oz. (78 gm.), **7M**; 51: 1½oz. (42 gm.), **8B**; 52: 1 lb. 7 oz. (655 gm.), **8C**; 53: 10 oz. (285 gm.), **7S**; †54: 2½ oz. (71 gm.), **7S**; †55: 2 oz. (57 gm.), **7S**; †56: 15 oz. (428 gm.), **7S**.

STONEMASONS' TOOLS (Fig. 31)

57. Mason's chisel with burred head and stem broadening out to the blade. Weight 6½ oz. (185 gm.). **8C**.
58. Wedge. The burred, rounded section head gives way to a tapering rectangular sectioned body whose feathered edges prevented the wedge jumping out of the stone when struck by a sledge-hammer. Two similar tools were found in a Roman context in the core of Hadrian's Wall on Brunton Bank, Northumberland.[1] Weight 11½ oz. (327 gm.). **7S**.
59. L-shaped object, possibly a feather from quarrying. Stone can be quarried by using either wedges and slats or plug and feathers,[2] and 59 resembles feathers shown in use at Clipsham quarry, Leicestershire (Rutland).[3] Weight 8 oz. (227 gm.). **8B**.
60. Rectangular sectioned mill-bill tapering to a narrow blade at each end. Held in a wooden handle called a thrift, it was used for dressing millstones.[4] Weight 4½ oz. (128 gm.). **8B**.

CARPENTERS' TOOLS (Fig. 32)

†61. Axe, weight 2 lb. 2 oz. (963 gm.). **8C**.
62. Tool with unevenly worn blade asymmetrically set in side view. The drawn-out, diamond-shaped tang prevented it turning in its handle. The wear on the blade suggests that it is a chisel rather than a screwdriver: it may be compared with a tool from a probable fifteenth/sixteenth-century site near Sawtry, Cambridgeshire (Huntingdonshire).[5] **8C**.
†63. Mortice chisel with hexagonal socket. Mercer notes that this type of chisel is, and was, generally socketed to allow for heavy mallet striking.[6] **7S**.
†64. Arcuate sectioned object with incomplete tang at one end and one turned through a right angle at the other. Unusually shaped for a draw knife or shave, the object

[1] Noel Shaw, 'Two iron rock wedges from Hadrian's Wall', *Archaeologia Aeliana*, 4th S, 36 (1958), 313–14, pl. XXXII.
[2] W. J. Arkell, *Oxford Stone* (London, 1947), pp. 60, 120–1, figs. 9 and 18.
[3] Donovan Purcell, *Cambridge Stone* (London, 1967), p. 45, pl. 16a.
[4] Stanley Freese, *Windmills and Millwrighting* (London, 1957), pp. 101–6, pl. 28.
[5] Stephen Moorhouse, 'Excavation of a moated site near Sawtry, Huntingdonshire', *Proc. Cambridge Antiquarian Society*, 63 (1971), 85, fig. 4.6.
[6] Henry C. Mercer, *Ancient Carpenters' Tools* (Doylestown, 1960), pp. 167–70, fig. 153.

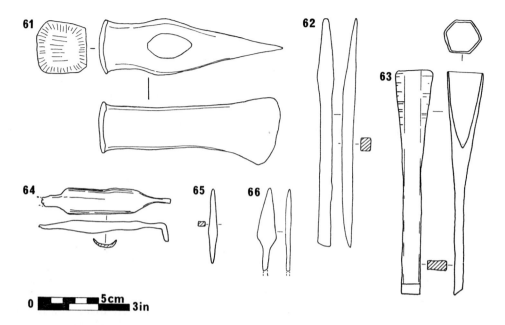

Fig. 32.   Chingley Forge. Iron: carpenters' tools. Periods II–III.   Scale: $\frac{1}{3}$

may be a fitting rather than a tool. A similar object is known from Sandal Castle, West Yorkshire (West Riding, Yorkshire).[1] **7S.**

65.   Awl, point lost, of rectangular section throughout. If a carpenter's brad awl, the point would have been chisel-shaped.[2] **7S.**

66.   Mood or blank for an auger bit. Six similar objects were found in a context with twelfth/thirteenth and sixteenth-century pottery at the forge at Waltham Abbey, Essex.[3] **8B.**

SPADE (Fig. 33)

67.   Spade of beech, the blade fitted with a spade-iron which has a worn rectangular mouth. The wooden blade fits into a V-shaped groove along the upper edge of the spade-iron, which has side-straps with nailed terminal lugs. At the head of the shaft is an incomplete D-shaped handle. The Chingley spade-iron, from a context of the very late sixteenth–seventeenth century, resembles one from a mid sixteenth-century context at Tattershall College, Lincolnshire, and another from Basing House, Hampshire,[4] occupied 1531–1645. **8G.**

STRUCTURAL IRONWORK (Fig. 34)

68.   Beam stirrup with base plate set at right angles to the side straps which are broken across nailholes. The stirrup supported timbers, especially joists, which ran at

---

[1] Excavated by P. Mayes. I should like to thank Mr W. L. Goodman for his comments on the above objects.
[2] Henry C. Mercer, op. cit., p. 67, note 6, pp. 176–7, fig. 160.
[3] Ian H. Goodall in P. J. and R. M. Huggins, 'Excavation of monastic forge and Saxo-Norman enclosure, Waltham Abbey, Essex, 1972–3', *Essex Archaeology and History*, 5 (1973), 170, fig. 11.12.
[4] Ian H. Goodall in Laurence Keen, 'Tattershall College; History and Excavation', forthcoming; Stephen Moorhouse and Ian H. Goodall in Stephen Moorhouse, op. cit., p. 61, n. 4, 43–4, fig. 19.55.

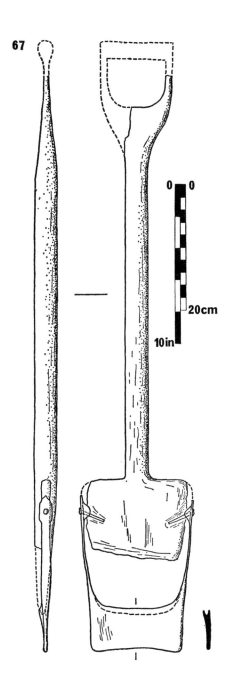

Fig. 33. Chingley Forge. Iron and wood spade. Period II. Scale: $\frac{1}{6}$

right-angles to other beams. Several of eighteenth-century date are known from the Fortress of Louisbourg, Nova Scotia, Canada.[1] **8B.**

69. Large rectangular headed staple, one arm broken. **7G.**
70, 71. Incomplete U-shaped staples. 70:**7S**, 71:**7G**. 71 *not illustrated.*
72. Rectangular headed staple, arm tips bent. **7S.**
73, 74. Hooks, similar in size to those used to hold an anvil to its block. **7S.**
75. Cotter pin. **8C.**
76, 77, 78, 79, 80. Washers, 76-8 flat, 79 and 80 thickening to the centre. 77 is 20-50 mm. diameter, 4 mm. thick; 78 is 23-58 mm. diameter, 3 mm. thick; 80 is 27-77 mm. diameter, 4-7 mm. thick. 76:**8B**, 77:**8C**, 78:**7A**, 79:**8C**, 80:**7P**, 77-8, 80 *not illustrated.*
81. Ring, circular in section. **8C.**
82. Slender timber dog. **7L.**
83. Eyed bar with tapering tang. **7G.**
84. Wallhook. **8C.**
85. Link, thinned and split at one end. **7M.**
86-8. Hinge pivots, 87 and 88 complete. Their sizes suggest their use for shutters and for doors of differing sizes; compare with others from Basing House, Hampshire.[2] 86:**7G**, 87:**7M**, 88:**8C.**
89. Curved bar of slightly tapered section with outer groove. Perhaps used with a pulley. **7S.**
90, 91, 92, 93. (*not illustrated*). Hinge straps, all fragmentary. 90: 220 mm. long, two nailholes, tapering from 27-19 mm. wide, 2 mm. thick. 91: 121 mm. long, two nailholes, one with a nail, tapering from 25-23 mm. in width, 4 mm. thick. 92: 840 mm. long, two nailholes, tapering from 24-20 mm. in width, 2 mm. thick. 93: 900 mm. long, broken across nailholes at each end, 43-39 mm. wide, 5 mm. thick. 90:**8B**, 91: **7S**, 92: **7M**, 93: **8C.**
94, 95, 96. Ribbed and perforated rectangular metal plates. 94 and 95 are of similar shape but 96 is only 90 × 60 mm., up to 4.5 mm. thick, and has one perforation. **7S** 95-6 *not illustrated.*

Nails: see section at end of Chingley Furnace metalwork report.

LOCKS AND KEYS (Fig. 35)

Barrel padlocks with shackles

Padlock bolts 97-100 are from barrel padlocks with shackles. In use they passed through the appropriately perforated end of the closed hinged shackle arm (cf. 101) into the padlock case, the springs opening once inside the padlock and thereby locking the arm in place. The arm was released by drawing a key along the bolt, closing the springs, and then ejecting it from the case. The distorted case from this type of padlock is known from a sixteenth-century context at the forge at Waltham Abbey, Essex,[3] but a complete example with its bolt, from Williamsburg, Virginia, is illustrated by Hume.[4]

97. Complete padlock bolt with two spines, each with a double leaf spring. One spring has a broader head which would complicate the ward cuts of its key. Unstratified.
†98. Padlock bolt with two spines, each with damaged springs. **8C.**

[1] John Dunton, *Building Hardware excavated at the Fortress of Louisbourg*, Manuscript Report no. 97, Parks Canada, Department of Indian Affairs and Northern Development (Louisbourg, 1972), pp. 211-13, figs. 103-4.
[2] Stephen Moorhouse and Ian H. Goodall in Stephen Moorhouse, op. cit., p. 61, note 4, 43, fig. 19.50-2.
[3] Ian H. Goodall in P. J. and R. M. Huggins, op. cit., p. 68, note 3, 170, fig. 11.28.
[4] Ivor Noël Hume, *A Guide to Artifacts of Colonial America* (New York, 1969), p. 249, fig. 78.1.

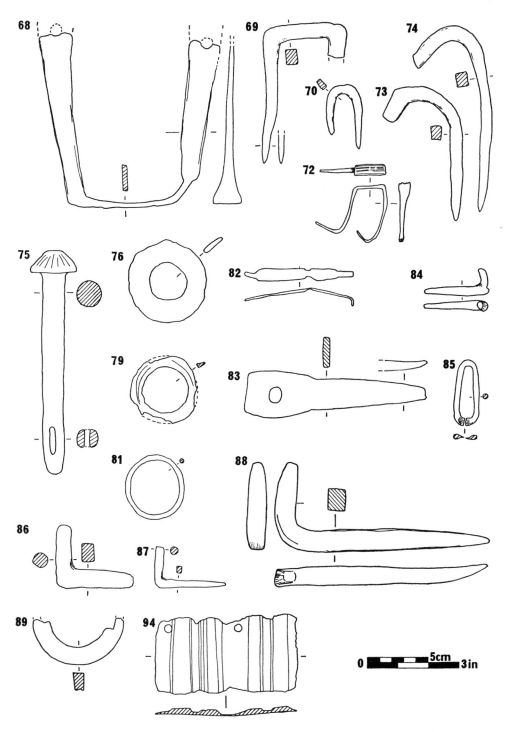

Fig. 34. Chingley Forge. Structural ironwork. Periods II–III. Scale: $\frac{1}{3}$

F

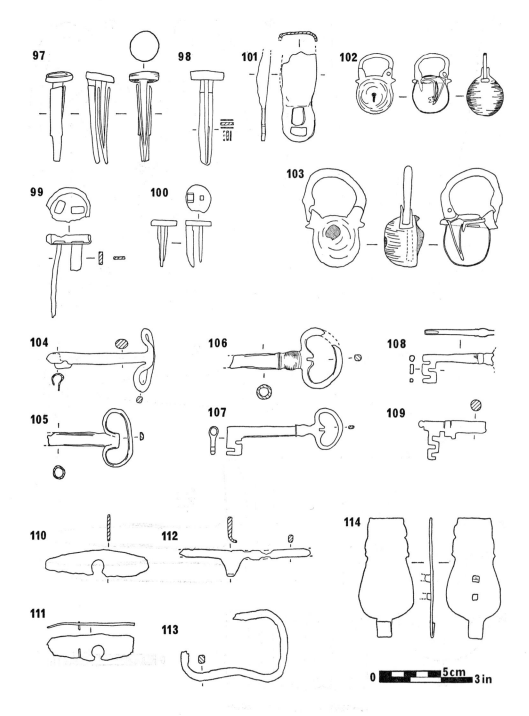

Fig. 35.   Chingley Forge. Iron: locks and keys. Periods II–III.   Scale: $\frac{1}{3}$.

99. Padlock bolt, head incomplete, the two spines broken. **7N.**
100. Padlock bolt, spines only. **7S.**
101. Bolt entry plate from the arm of a barrel padlock with shackle. **7S.**

Globular padlocks

The most common form of medieval padlock was the barrel padlock with a separate, inserted bolt which was released by a key drawn along the springs. At the close of the medieval period the padlock with a sliding bolt to engage the hasp, and worked by a revolving key, is found. A padlock hasp whose form implies its use with such a sliding bolt is known from a sixteenth-century context at Hadleigh Castle, Essex.[1] The two globular padlocks from Chingley, 102 and 103, worked on the same principle, each having had a key with a stem which projected beyond the bit. This projection located in a mount within the case of 102, and in a hole in the case of 103. To release the hinged hasp, the key had to slide the L-shaped bolt, normally held closed by the spring, out of its recessed end. Globular padlocks reached America in the first half of the seventeenth century, and have been found in contexts dating as late as 1730.[2]

*102. Complete globular padlock, corroded locked, with a keyhole in one side. **6A.**
†*103. Globular padlock, case incomplete, corroded unlocked. The keyhole has been lost, but the hole in which the tip of the key rested is present. **5F.**

Keys

The kidney-shaped bow, found during the late medieval period, is also one of the forms current during the sixteenth and seventeenth centuries. Bows similar to those of 104 and 105 come from post-medieval contexts at Basing House, Hampshire; Sandal Castle, West Yorkshire (West Riding, Yorkshire); and Humberstone, Leicester,[3] whilst the split internal projection of 106 and 107 is found on a key from a late fifteenth/early sixteenth-century context at Somerby, Lincolnshire, from Basing House, Hampshire and from a probable post-medieval context at Montgomery Castle, Powys (Montgomeryshire).[4] The mouldings on the stems of 106–9, although found on some medieval keys, are a more characteristically post-medieval feature.

104. Key with distorted kidney-shaped bow and solid stem becoming hollow at the fragmentary bit. **7L.**
105. Key with kidney-shaped bow and broken, hollow stem. **6A.**
106. Key, incomplete kidney-shaped bow with internal moulding, moulded stem, hollow at the break. **8B.**
107. Key, similar to 106, but with partially hollow stem. **8C.**
108. Key, solid moulded stem, broken bow. **7S.**
*109. Fragment of key stem and bit. **8B.**

Locks and Hasps

110, 111. Amongst the individual parts of door-mounted locks were the wards, shaped plates of metal which the bit of the key had to pass before finally throwing the bolt.

[1] Ian H. Goodall in P. L. Drewett, 'Excavations at Hadleigh Castle, Essex', *Journal of the British Archaeological Association*, 38 (1975), forthcoming.
[2] Ivor Noël Hume, op. cit., p. 70, note 4, p. 250.
[3] Stephen Moorhouse and Ian H. Goodall in Stephen Moorhouse, op. cit., p. 61 note 4, 39–41, figs. 18.22, 33, 34; Sandal Castle: excavated by P. Mayes; P. A. Rahtz, 'Humberstone Earthwork, Leicester', *Trans. Leicestershire Archaeological and Historical Society*, 35 (1959), 17, fig. 14.15.
[4] D. C. Mynard, 'Excavations at Somerby, Lincs., 1957', *Lincolnshire History and Archaeology*, 4 (1969), 83, fig. 12 I.W.75; Stephen Moorhouse and Ian H. Goodall in Stephen Moorhouse, op. cit., p. 61, note 4, 39–41, fig. 18.25; J. M. Lewis, 'The Excavation of the "New Building" at Montgomery Castle', *Archaeologia Cambrensis*, 117 (1968), 149, fig. 8.5.

The ends of the wards were either mounted in wood or in metal plates attached to the lock case. The plain ward, 110, was passed by vertical ward cuts in the key bit, the additional collar on 111 by horizontal cuts. Similar wards have been found in medieval and later contexts, and complete locks of seventeenth and eighteenth-century date are illustrated by Hume.[1] 110:**8C**, 111:**7S**.

112. Sliding door bolt. **7S.**
113. Hasp loop. **5F.**
114. Hasp, hinged top lost and rear D-staple broken. Perhaps from a chest. **6A.**

HORSE FURNITURE (Fig. 36)

Horses' bits

The difference between snaffle and curb bits lies principally in the form of their cheekpieces. Those of the snaffle bit have a loop which takes both the mouthpiece and reins, whereas the curb bit's has additional loops and fittings to take the reins and other straps and chains. 115 is a common medieval[2] and later type of snaffle bit cheekpiece: post-medieval examples include those from the 1645 forge at Sandal Castle, West Yorkshire (West Riding, Yorkshire) and one from Virginia discarded *c.* 1730.[3] 116 and 117 resemble bits from Basing House, Hampshire and from the 1645 forge at Sandal Castle, West Yorkshire (West Riding, Yorkshire), in addition to one from Virginia discarded *c.* 1730.[4] Both have holes through which the bridle bosses were fixed. 118 is one of the more elaborate forms of mouthpiece from a curb bit.

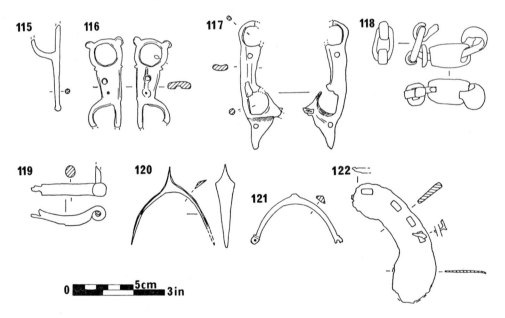

Fig. 36. Chingley Forge. Iron: horse furniture. Periods II–III. Scale: $\frac{1}{3}$

[1] Ivor Noël Hume, op. cit., p. 70, note 4, pp. 243–8.
[2] *London Museum Medieval Catalogue* (London, 1967 edition), pp. 80–5.
[3] Sandal Castle: excavated by P. Mayes; Ivor Noël Hume, op. cit., p. 70, note 4, p. 241, fig. 75.3.
[4] Stephen Moorhouse and Ian H. Goodall in Stephen Moorhouse, op. cit., p. 61, note 4, 47–9, fig. 21.89; Sandal Castle: excavated by P. Mayes; Ivor Noël Hume, op. cit., p. 70, note 4, p. 241, fig. 75.5.

115. Incomplete snaffle bit cheekpiece. **3C.**

*116. Upper part of the cheekpiece from a curb bit. The upper of the two holes, which retains some copper alloy, held the top mount of the bridle boss; the lower hole probably held a swivel hook which carried a strap or chain round the back of the horse's jaw. **7S.**

117. Upper part of a curb bit cheekpiece with two holes for attaching the bridle boss. The lower part of the cheekpiece ran from the corner of the D-loop. **8B.**

*118. Part of a curb bit mouthpiece with a melon-shaped tube around the complete link. **7S.**

119. Fragmentary bit cheekpiece and mouthpiece link. **4N.**

Spurs By BLANCHE ELLIS

†120. The severely rusted remains of an iron spur body. In its present condition precise identification is impossible, but its small size and general proportions are those of a type of rowel spur in common use in England in the second half of the seventeenth century. Such spurs often had sides which tapered from their deepest part behind the wearer's heels as appears to have been the case with the spur under discussion. Their necks were small, fairly straight, carrying small rowels. The neck of 120 has rusted away to a pointed stump and the terminals of the sides have completely disappeared. **7S.**

*121. Fragment of a severly corroded iron spur body. The neck has completely rusted away and the front parts of the hinged sides are missing. All that remains is the small arc of metal which goes around the back of the wearer's foot ending at each side in a circular, vertically pierced projection. These projections are part of the hinges to which the front pieces of the sides were attached by pins. One of the hinge pins, possibly both, are still in position in the holes.

From medieval times spurs were occasionally made with a hinge in one or in both of their sides, making possible some adjustment in fitting to the boot. At the end of the seventeenth century and during the eighteenth century in western Europe including England, large, rather solid and inflexible leather riding boots were worn and spurs with hinged sides became quite common. Robert Plot[1] recorded the making of 'joynted' spur bodies at Walsall in Staffordshire which he visited in 1680, and in 1763 Diderot[2] illustrated eight contemporary spurs, four of which had hinged sides. One cannot therefore date the Chingley Forge fragment more closely than by the archaeological evidence of the site. An X-ray photograph reveals traces of non-ferrous plating and one hinge pin (?non-ferrous) still in place. Throughout their history iron spurs were often tinned;[3] sometimes silver decoration was applied to spurs. The moving parts of iron spurs such as rowel pins or hinge pins were sometimes made of copper alloy. **4N.**

Oxshoe

122. Oxshoe, four nail-holes, one with the fragment of a large rectangular-headed nail in place. Base of upturned clip, broadened and flattened heel. A similarly shaped oxshoe was found with seventeenth-century objects at Hangleton, West Sussex

---

[1] Robert Plot, *The Natural History of Stafford-shire* (Oxford, 1686), pp. 376–7.
[2] Denis Diderot and Jean le Rond d'Alembert (editors), *Encyclopédie ou Dictionnaire Raisonné des Sciences, des Arts et des Métiers* (Paris, 1751–77), Section: Eperonnier, published 1763, pl. xv.
[3] E. M. Jope, 'The Tinning of Iron Spurs: A Continuous Practice from the Tenth to the Seventeenth Century', *Oxoniensia*, 21 (1956), 35–42.

(Sussex), and oxshoes from the 1645 forge at Sandal Castle, West Yorkshire (West Riding, Yorkshire)[1] have long rectangular nails. 7Q.

WEAPONS AND ARMOUR *By* ALAN BORG (Figs. 37, 38)

†37:123. Sword pommel, hollow, forged in a single piece, and roughly egg-shaped. The decoration consists of vertical bands of foliage, with alternate bands pierced. In the pierced bands the foliage scrolls are inhabited by human figures and dragons' heads. The quality of the chiselled decoration is high and the pommel clearly comes from a very fine sword.

The size, shape, and decoration of the pommel indicate that it is from a rapier of the first half of the seventeenth century. Specific connexions can be drawn in with a group of rapiers, usually regarded as English and dating from *c.* 1610–30.[2] The pommels of

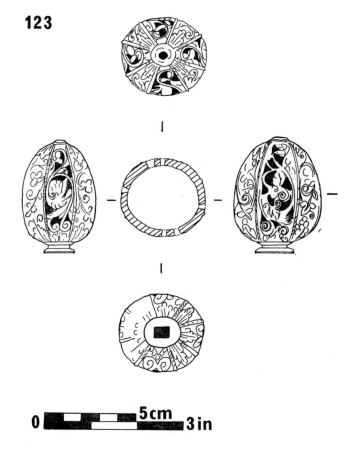

Fig. 37. Chingley Forge. Iron: rapier pommel. Periods II–III.

Scale: ½

---

[1] E. W. Holden, 'Excavations at the Deserted Medieval Village of Hangleton, Part I', *Sussex Archaeological Collections*, 101 (1963), 173, fig. 38.12; Sandal Castle: excavated by P. Mayes.
[2] For example, Tower of London Armouries Class IX–899.

these swords compare in size and shape with the present example, and are also decorated with bands of foliage, usually inlaid with silver. However, the pommels on such swords are solid and hollow pierced pommels are more characteristic of continental workmanship.[1] The style of the decoration on the pommel cannot, in the present state of knowledge, be localized, but it can be suggested that the pommel comes from a rapier hilt of English or German manufacture, and dates *c.* 1610–30. **7S.**

†38:124. Ovoid pommel and section of tang from a sword or rapier, probably dating from the second or third quarters of the seventeenth century. There is no screw hole or

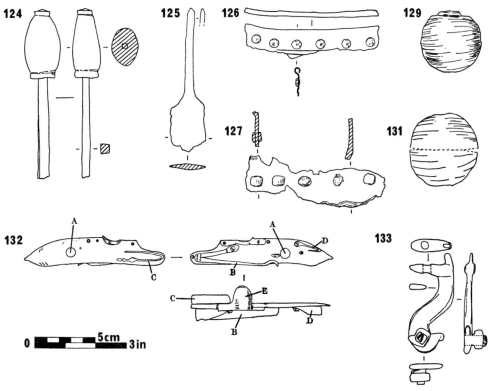

132:

(A) Hole for the axle and tumbler of the cock which held the flint.
(B) Mainspring which acted on the cock.
(C) Frizzle or steel spring.
    The frizzle was a right-angled piece of steel; the horizontal part acting as a pan-cover, the upright piece as the steel against which the flint struck to produce the necessary sparks.
(D) Sear Spring.
    The sear caught in notches cut in the tumbler and held the cock in its cocked or firing position until released by pressure of the trigger.
(E) The pan holding the priming powder. When the lock was screwed to the gun the priming pan lay next to the touchhole of the barrel.

Fig. 38. Chingley Forge. Iron: weapons, armour, firearms, cannon ball.
Periods II–III. Scale: ⅓

[1] For example, Paris, Musee de l'Armée J.138, a German rapier *c.* 1600.

slot in the pommel to receive a knuckle bow. Such flattened ovoid pommels were commonly used in the seventeenth century, and no firm date or place of origin can be given for this specimen. **5F.**

125.   Tang and upper portion of blade from a short dagger. The blade is of flattened diamond section, and there is no ricasso, suggesting that the weapon was not intended for rapier and dagger fencing — left-hand daggers normally have a ricasso. The specimen is too fragmentary to allow any dating to be given. **7K.**

126.   Fragment from an armour plate. This piece, with its turned, roped edge and row of rivets is clearly from a portion of body armour, and the curvature suggests that it could well be part of the top lame of a pauldron. Alternatively, the piece could have been flattened, and originally have formed the cuff edge of a gauntlet. The comparatively large number of rivets suggest a seventeenth-century date, and it is probable that every other rivet was merely decorative. It should date from the first half of the seventeenth century. **7S.**

127.   The specimen is too fragmentary for a firm identification, but it could be a fragment of a lame from an armour of the first half of the seventeenth century. **8C.**

CANNON BALLS AND GRENADE (Fig. 38)

†*128.   Cannon ball, 47.5 mm. diameter, weight 15 oz. (426 gm.). **7S.**   *Not illustrated.*

129.   Cannon ball, 48.5 mm. diameter, weight $15\frac{1}{2}$ oz. (433 gm.). **7S.**

130.   Cannon ball, 89.5 mm. diameter, weight 5 lb. $12\frac{1}{2}$ oz. (2622 gm.). **7S.**   *Not illustrated.*

†131.   Spherical object, 58 mm. diameter, made in two halves, the 2 mm.-thick wrought-iron hemispheres brazed together. The contents were largely hydrated iron oxide, but it was not clear if this was an original filling or a deposit from iron-bearing water seeping in through the damaged joint. It could thus be either a form of grenade, or a metal 'boule' as of the kind used in the French game. **7S.**

FIREARMS *By* H. L. BLACKMORE (Fig. 38)

†*132.   Gun-lock. This is the remains of a flintlock, the cock, tumbler and steel being missing. The shape of the plate (usually compared to a banana) and the absence of bridles inside and out, date the lock to the late-seventeenth-early eighteenth century. It is a type and size of lock found on English pocket pistols of this period. See caption to Fig. 38 for an explanation of the function of the surviving parts of the lock. **7S.**

*133.   Gun-cock. This type of cock appears on English guns of the late sixteenth century and continued in use during the first two decades of the seventeenth century. The type of lock associated with this cock is one in which the steel is separate from the pan-cover and is known today as a snaphaunce, although contemporarily the word simply meant any lock using a flint and steel for ignition. The cock is distinguished by its long neck and the short tail or heel which acted as a catch for a horizontally-acting sear protruding through the lock plate. It is found on English pistols dated 1601 at Levens Hall, Cumbria (Westmorland) and on a number of English pistols in the Palazzo Ducale, Venice. **7S.**

The gun-cock, 133, comes from a period when firearms were often made locally rather than in known firearm-manufacturing centres of London and Birmingham. They were often of quite crude construction and it may well be that the Kent and Sussex iron forges were responsible for the supply of rough parts to the lock-makers elsewhere or, of course, they could have made the complete locks. The gun-lock, 132, however, is of good quality and at the time of its manufacture the lock-making industry was firmly established in London. Nevertheless it was not unknown for fine quality firearms to be produced in small towns or villages by otherwise unknown gunmakers. There is, however, no record of such a gunmaker working in Lamberhurst, neither is there any known instance of locks being purchased here by the trade.

Box Irons (Fig. 39)

Box irons 134–6 are all of the same shape, although the layout of their basal grids differs. The form of the handles of 134 and 135 also differs, that of 134 resembling 138 and 139. The wall and door fragment, 137, indicates that the irons were constructed by joining separate top and base plates to a wall which was strengthened with several vertical ribs. These ribs, on 137, project beyond the edges of the wall and, unless they were sawn off, could have fitted into recesses in the other plates and thus have given rigidity to the whole case. A sliding bolt, held by staples to the outside of the hinged door, must have engaged in a catch projecting from the side of the box iron.

Box irons were heated by inserting an iron block or heater whose heat was transferred to the base-plate through geometrically arranged thin iron strips. A number of similar box irons are known from eighteenth-century contexts in Virginia, as also are several variously shaped heaters.[1] Most heaters were from eighteenth-century contexts, but one came unstratified from the mid seventeenth-century Mathews Manor in Warwick County.

134. Box iron with gridded base, door with bolt, incomplete handle. Unstratified.
135. Box iron with scrolled base, door with bolt, broken handle. **5A.**
†136. Base and wall of a box iron of similar shape to 134 and 135. 126 mm. long, 95 mm. wide, with a wall 40 mm. high, the basal grid comprises a long strip down much of the centre of the case crossed at right angles by two shorter strips. **8C.** *Not illustrated.*
137. Fragment of the wall and door of a box iron. The wall fragment, 190 mm. long, 35 mm. tall, 3 mm. thick, has two vertical ribs, each 39 mm. long, attached to its inner face. The door, which is hinged but as yet lacks a sliding closure bolt, is 65 mm. long by 25 mm. by 2 mm. **75.** *Not illustrated.*
138. Decorated handle from a box iron. **7S.**
139. Plain handle, similar to 138, with incomplete terminals. **7S.** *Not illustrated.*

Buckles (Fig. 40)

140. Incomplete rectangular buckle frame. **7S.**
141. Rectangular buckle, pin lost. **8H/8E.**
142. Incomplete D-shaped buckle. **5F.**
143. Rectangular buckle with central bar, curved in top view. Pin lost. **7S.**

Cast Iron Vessels (Fig. 40)

The various cast iron pieces may be compared with more complete examples, some of differing dates and metals, figured by Seymour Lindsay.[2] Excavated examples include those from Riplingham, Humberside (East Riding, Yorkshire) and Woodhouse, West Felton, Salop.[3]

144. Fragment of the rim and body, down to the carination, of a finely cast cauldron. **7S.**
145. Vessel body fragment. **5F.**
146–8. Vessel legs or feet of various forms. 146, 147:**7S**, †148:**5F.**

---

[1] Unpublished. I am grateful to Mr I. Noël Hume for providing details of them.
[2] J. Seymour Lindsay, *Iron and Brass Implements of the English House* (London, 1964 edition), pp. 25–7, figs. 111–24, 127.
[3] J. Wacher, 'Excavations at Riplingham, East Yorkshire, 1956–7', *Yorkshire Archaeological Journal*, 41 (1966), 660–2, fig. 26; T. W. Rogers, 'Vessels and Armour at Woodhouse, West Felton', *Trans. Shropshire Archaeological Society*, 56 (1960), 343–5.

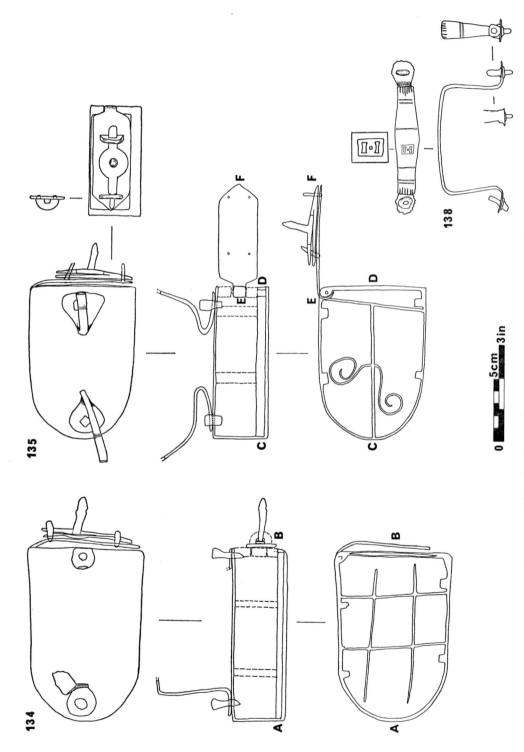

Fig. 39.   Chingley Forge. Iron: box irons. Periods II–III.   Scale: ⅓

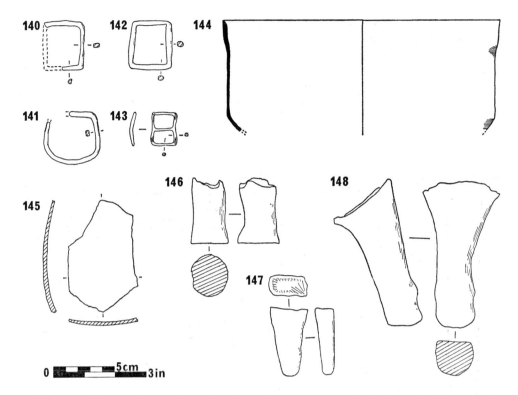

Fig. 40. Chingley Forge. Iron: buckles and cast iron vessels. Periods II–III. Scale ⅓

149. Slightly tapering, hexagonal sectioned leg. 73 mm. long, 24 × 17 mm. maximum cross-section. **7S.** *Not illustrated.*

MISCELLANEOUS IRON OBJECTS (Fig. 41)

150. Tube of tapering circular section becoming triangular at the narrower end. Formed by bending round and butting an iron sheet, the tube has six holes facing differing directions in its narrower part. A hole at the broader end is likely to have been caused by corrosion. The tube may have been used with a pair of bellows. **8C.**

151. Tapering tube in two pieces, one with a hole. **8B.**

†152. Tube, closed at one end, with an eye mounted on the back. **7S.**

*153. Hinge loop of a pair of calipers, each arm tapering at its head immediately above a locating nib. **4P.**

154. Curving arm with shaped terminal. **7S.**

155. Lug. **7S.**

†156. Square nut with central screw thread. **7S.**

†*157. Cog corroded on to an incomplete object. **8B.**

158. Fishhook with expanded head to retain the line. Barbed hook lost. **9E.**

159. Sheet iron disc with riveted eye and thickened strip for hinge. Probably a lid. **7S.**

160–2. Three sheet iron fragments. 160: 105 mm. diameter with a central rectangular hole. 161: at least 85 mm. diameter with a small rectangular lug and random perforations.

162: incomplete rectangle, 127 × 50 mm. maximum, with perforated, projecting lug. **7S.** *Not illustrated.*

163.   Fragment of a cast iron grate. **7S.**

164–6.   Broken cast iron racks or ratchet bars. 166 is a broken piece 143 mm. long with teeth of similar size to 164. 164–5:**7S**, 166:**5F.** *Not illustrated.*

*167.   Rectangular strap with two-piece cross fitting, one arm perforated, set at one end. **7S.**

168.   Jew's harp, reed and one arm broken. **8C.**

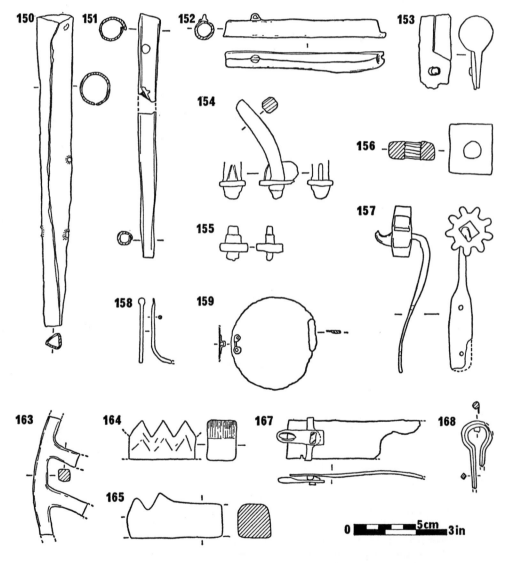

Fig. 41.   Chingley Forge. Miscellaneous iron objects. Periods II–III.   Scale: ⅓

COPPER ALLOY OBJECTS: Periods II and III (Fig. 42)

1. Spatulate spoon terminal with upturned hook and the letters E F stamped on the face. Spatulate terminals, generally notched to create a trifid end, were popular in the second half of the seventeenth century, and by the end of the century there had developed the type with a wavy end whose central projection often turned up into a hook. Both types of terminal survived into the early nineteenth century, but by about 1715 the rounded end, still upturned towards the face, was fashionable. In the 1760s the end of the stem became down-turned.[1] The Chingley Forge spoon terminal most closely resembles the rounded type with upturned hook. **7S.**

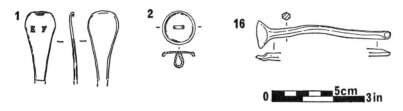

Fig. 42. Chingley Forge. Copper alloy (1, 2) and lead alloy (16) objects. Periods II–III. Scale: ⅓

2. Button, slightly raised disc with chamfered edge, the eye formed from a strip of metal bent into a hook and soldered in position at one end. **7Q.**

†3. Pin with double twist head. 21.5 mm. long, complete. **7S.** *Not illustrated.*

†4–5. Pins with globular heads, 25 mm. long, complete, **7S** and **8C.**

6–8. 6 and 7 are sheet metal patches with rivets, like 8 of similar thickness sheet. 6, with eleven rivets, is an internal corner patch from a leather container, whereas 7, which is flat and has perforations close to the edge which retain two rivets, may be from a repair of either a leather or a metal object. 6: unstratified, 7:**7M**; 8:**7S.**

9–14. Pieces of scrap. 9 is a piece of sheet with two holes, 10 and 11 have clear shear cuts, and 12 is a rectangular strip. 13 consists of two small coils of 5 mm. wide strip, and 14 is a further curved length of scrap. 9–12:**7S**, 13:**3C**, 14:**5E.** *Not illustrated.*

†15. Object resembling the gate, or waste metal, from a casting, or possibly a rivet. An 8 mm. long, 6 × 7 mm. oval-section stem runs from a distorted 18 × 24 mm. head, maximum thickness 4 mm. **7S.** *Not illustrated.*

LEAD ALLOY OBJECTS: Periods II and III (Fig. 42)

16. Medieval and certain later spoons had stems which terminated in ornamental finials, but by the end of the fifteenth century the stem with an obliquely cut off end was known. Known as the 'slipped end' type, it was made at least as late as 1657.[2] The Chingley Forge spoon has the characteristic hexagonal section stem and a circular depression in the cut end. The bowl is incomplete. **8B.**

[1] F. G. Hilton Price, *Old Base Metal Spoons* (London, 1908), pp. 42–7; Ivor Noël Hume, op. cit., p. 70, note 4, p. 183.
[2] F. G. Hilton Price, ibid., pp. 38–41; Ivor Noël Hume, op. cit., p. 70, note 4, p. 181.

G

17. Lead sheet 207 × 152 mm. 2 mm. thick, with rows of five and seven nailholes close to the two shorter sides, and three rows of two between. Depressions in the lead show heads of nails, generally rounded and up to 15 mm. diameter, but occasionally square, with shanks 3 × 4 mm. **8B.**   *Not illustrated.*

18–19. Scrap. 18 is a 172 mm. long piece of window came of H-section, 3 × 3 mm. maximum cross-section, bent into a coil. 19 is a formless lump. 18:**7S**, 19:**3C.** *Not illustrated.*

CHINGLEY FURNACE METALWORK *By* IAN H. GOODALL

IRON OBJECTS (Figs. 43, 44)

43:1. Long narrow chisel, tapered to blade and burred head. Weight 7 oz. (199 gm.) **5.**

   2. Chisel with burred head. Weight 14½ oz. (412 gm.) **33.**

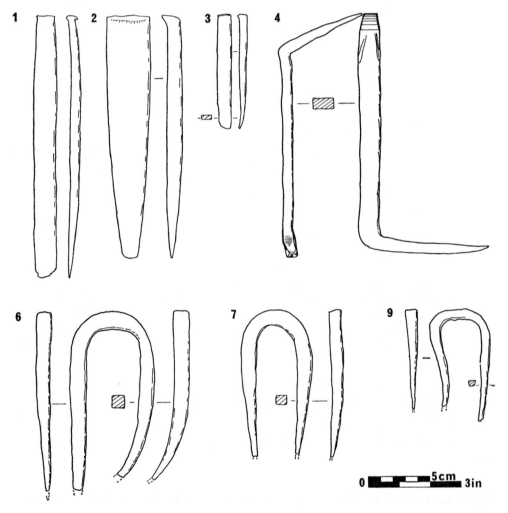

Fig. 43.   Chingley Furnace. Iron objects.   Scale: ⅓

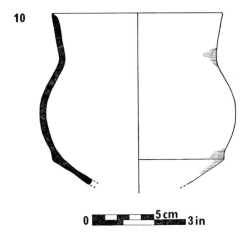

Fig. 44. Chingley Furnace. Cast Iron Pot. Scale: ⅓

3. Chisel with slightly burred head. Weight 1½ oz. (50 gm.) **33**.

4, 5. Two similarly shaped ties for holding the two fulcrum posts to the cross sleeper of the bellows foundation. The two spikes at the ends of each tie, though in the same plane, are set at right angles to each other. Both **29**. 5 *not illustrated*.

6–9. Large U-shaped staples, various arms incomplete. 5, and to a lesser degree 4, has an internal shaping. All **29**.

†44:10. Fragment of a small, cast iron cauldron. **4**.

NAILS FROM CHINGLEY FORGE AND CHINGLEY FURNACE *By* IAN H. GOODALL

TIMBER NAILS (Fig. 45)

The nails from Chingley Forge Period I, from Periods II and III, and from Chingley Furnace are discussed separately after each type has been described. All nails have square or rectangular sectioned shanks. Lengths refer to complete examples unless stated otherwise; shank dimensions have been taken immediately below the head but away from any distortion which this has caused. The range of types may be compared with those from the forge at Waltham Abbey, Essex, and from Basing House, Hampshire.[1]

Type 1. Headless nail.
    Forge, Period I: 38–52 mm. long, tops 2 × 4 to 3 × 5 mm.
    Forge, Periods II and III: 33–85 mm. long, tops 3 × 4 to 7 × 8 mm.
    Furnace: 56–85 mm. long, tops 5 × 5 to 7 × 8 mm.
Type 2. Head formed by a flaring shank, the larger ones wedge-shaped.
    Forge, Period I: 27–42 mm. long, heads 1 × 6 to 2 × 8 mm.
    Forge, Periods II and III: 51–84 mm. long, heads 6 × 7 to 13 × 17 mm.
Type 3. Flat rectangular head overlapping a wedge-shaped shank.
    Forge, Period I: 39–59 mm. long, heads 4 × 6 to 7 × 10 mm., shanks 2 × 4 to 4 × 6 mm.
    Forge, Periods II and III: 61–90 mm. long, heads 10 × 12 to 13 × 18 mm., shank 10 × 12 mm.
    Furnace: 81 mm. long, head 13 × 13 mm., shank 8 × 8 mm.

[1] Ian H. Goodall in P. J. and R. M. Huggins, op. cit., p. 68, note 3, 175, fig. 13; Stephen Moorhouse and Ian H. Goodall in Stephen Moorhouse, op. cit., p. 61, note 4, 49–51, fig. 22.90–111.

Type 4.   L-shaped head no wider than the tang.

    Forge, Periods II–III: 116 mm. long, head 6 × 14 mm., shank 6 × 7 mm.

Type 5.   Flat, figure-8 shaped head.

    Forge, Period I: 36–77 mm. long, heads 3 × 6 to 15 × 22 mm., shanks 2 × 4 to 5 × 7 mm.

    Forge, Periods II–III: 21–94 mm. long, heads 2 × 6 to 7 × 13 mm., shanks 2 × 3 to
      3 × 5 mm.

Type 6.   Long flat rectangular head not wider than twice the width of the shank, length
    variable.

    Forge, Period I: 48 mm. long, incomplete, heads 6 × 11 to 6 × 16 mm., shanks 3 × 4 to
      5 × 6 mm.

    Forge, Period II–III: 41 mm. long, head 6 × 10 mm., shank 3 × 6 mm.

    Furnace: 36–59 mm. long, heads 11 × 18 to 14 × 20 mm., shanks 3 × 4 to 3 × 5 mm.

Type 7.   Square or rectangular head, often with rounded corners. Head flat or slightly raised,
    some approaching Type 8.

    Forge, Period I: 27–108 mm. long, heads 6 × 7 to 23 × 25 mm., shanks 2 × 2 to
      6 × 8 mm.

    Forge, Periods II–III: 46–134 mm. long, heads 6 × 7 to 23 × 26 mm. shanks 2 × 3 to
      7 × 8 mm.

    Furnace: 46–65 mm. long, heads 10 × 11 to 18 × 18 mm., shanks 3 × 3 to 4 × 5 mm.

Type 8.   Pyramidal, rectangular head.

    Forge, Periods II–III: 103 mm. long, head 12 × 12 mm., 4 mm. deep, shank 3 × 5 mm.

    Furnace: 54–79 mm. long, heads 10 × 12 to 13 × 20 mm., 3–4 mm. deep, shanks 3 × 4 to
      3 × 5 mm.

Type 9.   Long rectangular head raised to ridge across head.

    Forge, Periods II–III: 41 mm. long, head 5 × 8 mm., 2 mm. deep, shank 3 × 4 mm.

    Furnace: 44–65 mm. long, heads 9 × 15 to 10 × 21 mm., 3 mm. deep, shanks 3 × 3 to
      3 × 6 mm.

Type 10.   Long rectangular head, domed.

    Forge, Periods II–III: 103 mm. long, incomplete, heads 13 × 24 to 18 × 39 mm.,
      6 mm. deep, shanks 9 × 10 to 8 × 14 mm.

Type 11.   Rounded or circular domed head.

    Forge, Periods II–III: 46–138 mm. long, heads 10 × 11 to 22 × 30 mm., shanks 3 × 4 to
      5 × 11 mm.

Type 12.   Square or rectangular head with chamfered corners.

    Forge, Periods II–III: 144–230 mm. long, heads 15 × 16 to 27 × 28 mm., 4–10 mm. deep,
    shanks 5 × 10 to 10 × 12 mm.

Type 13.   Studs, square or rectangular heads.

    Forge, Periods II–III: 74 mm. long, incomplete, heads 23 × 50 to 34 × 41 mm.
    (incomplete), 6–8 mm. deep, shanks 9 × 13 to 10 × 13 mm.

CHINGLEY FORGE PERIOD I

Type	1	2	3	4	5	6	7	8	9	10	11	12	13	Total
Context 9C	—	—	2	—	—	—	16	—	—	—	—	—	—	18
9E	11	14	17	—	3	2	93	—	—	—	—	—	—	140
TOTAL	11	14	19	—	3	2	109	—	—	—	—	—	—	158

CHINGLEY FORGE PERIODS II AND III

Type	1	2	3	4	5	6	7	8	9	10	11	12	13	Total
Context 5F	—	—	—	—	—	—	4	—	—	—	—	—	—	4
8C	—	1	—	—	3	—	51	—	—	2	7	1	—	65
8D	—	—	—	—	—	2	—	—	—	—	—	—	—	2
8B	—	2	—	—	—	—	18	—	—	1	1	—	1	23
7A	—	—	—	—	—	—	6	—	—	—	—	—	1	7
7F	—	1	—	—	—	—	5	—	—	—	—	3	—	9
7G	—	—	1	—	—	—	16	—	—	—	2	9	—	28
7K	—	—	—	—	—	—	—	—	—	—	—	1	—	1
7M	—	2	1	—	—	—	4	—	—	—	1	2	—	10
7N	—	1	—	—	—	—	3	—	—	—	—	—	—	4
7P	—	—	—	—	—	—	5	—	—	—	1	—	—	6
7Q	—	—	—	—	—	—	1	—	—	—	—	—	—	1
7R	—	—	—	—	—	—	6	—	—	—	—	—	—	6
7S	14	1	—	1	4	—	118	1	2	—	60	14	—	215
4N	—	—	—	—	—	—	—	—	—	—	2	2	—	4
5A	—	—	—	—	—	—	1	—	—	—	1	—	—	2
TOTAL	14	8	2	1	7	2	238	1	2	3	75	32	2	387

CHINGLEY FURNACE

Type	1	2	3	4	5	6	7	8	9	10	11	12	13	Total
Context 29	11	—	1	—	—	15	12	3	33	—	—	—	—	75
33	—	—	—	—	—	—	3	2	4	—	—	—	—	9
34	—	—	—	—	—	—	2	1	1	—	—	—	—	4
28	—	—	—	—	—	2	2	—	8	—	—	—	—	12
TOTAL	11	—	1	—	—	17	19	6	46	—	—	—	—	100

HORSESHOE NAILS (Fig. 45)

Measurements are subject to the criteria used for timber nails, noted above. Shanks are square or rectangular. Type A horseshoe nails are from Forge, Period I, types B–D from Forge, Periods II and III. Types A and B are related to medieval horseshoe nails with trapezoidal heads and often well-marked ears, and some examples are included in the type B nails from the forge at Waltham Abbey, Essex. Types C and D are known from late medieval and post-medieval contexts.[1]

Type A.   Rectangular head flaring to the top in the longer dimension, expanded and then tapered in the other.
Forge, Period I: 23 mm. long, incomplete, heads 6 × 12 mm., shanks 4 × 4 mm.

[1] For a fuller discussion of horseshoe nails see Ian H. Goodall in P. J. and R. M. Huggins, op. cit., p. 68, note 3, 173–5, fig. 13.

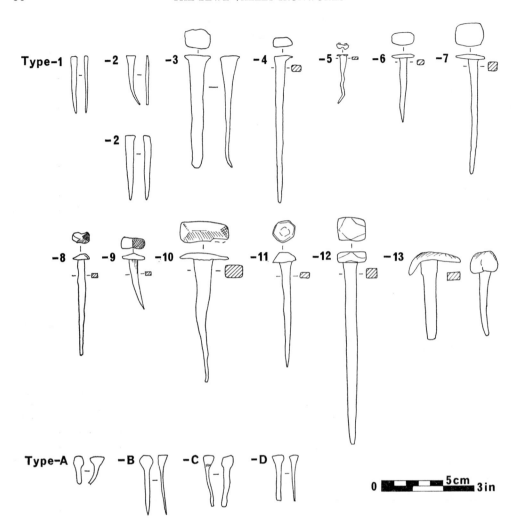

Fig. 45.   Chingley Forge and Furnace. Iron nail types.   Scale: $\frac{1}{3}$

Type B.   Rectangular head flaring to the top in the shorter dimension, expanded and then
    tapered in the other.
    Forge, Periods II–III: 34–47 mm. long, head tops 5 × 9 to 7 × 11 mm., shanks 1 × 3 to
    2 × 5 mm.

Type C.   Shouldered head with straight sides, expanding in side view.
    Forge, Periods II–III: 50 mm. long, heads 8 × 8., shanks 3 × 5 mm.

Type D.   Head formed by the shank expanding from all sides up to the flat top.
    Forge, Periods II–III: 39 mm. long, incomplete, heads 6 × 8 to 9 × 9 mm., shanks
    2 × 3 to 2 × 4 mm.

Type		A	B	C	D	Total
Context	9E	2	—	—	—	2
	5F	—	1	—	1	2
	8C	—	1	—	4	5
	8B	—	—	—	1	1
	7A	—	—	—	2	2
	7M	—	—	1	1	2
	7S	—	9	1	12	22
TOTAL		2	11	2	21	36

THE COINS

By GEOFFREY D. LEWIS

CHINGLEY FORGE

Layer 7S

Copper halfpenny of William III. In poor condition with most of legend and date obliterated. This type was minted during the years 1695–1701 and this particular coin is almost certainly dated 1699.

Ledger 3C

This piece is too corroded to identify positively. It is, however, of copper and of farthing form. Certain features would not be incompatible with farthings minted by Charles II between 1672–6 and in 1679.

VII   Examination of Metal Artifacts from Chingley Forge and Furnace

By DR R. F. TYLECOTE

The specimens were examined by cutting out suitable sections, polishing them in the normal metallographic manner using diamond abrasives, and in the case of the ferrous artifacts etching in nital. The non-ferrous specimens were etched in ferric chloride. All hardness-test numbers are Vickers HV5 (5 kg. load) except where otherwise stated (HV1, 2.5 etc.) All items are from Chingley Forge except where indicated.

BLADES

KNIVES

PERIOD I

Fig. 27:1.   Knife blade. A homogeneous steel blade of tempered martensite. Hardness near cutting edge, 533; at back of blade the same (532). This type is unusual for such an early period.

Fig. 27:2.   Knife. Hard. Steel edged; well diffused. Edge, tempered martensite. Rest, ferrite and pearlite.

PERIODS II–III

Generally the knives were made of homogeneous carbon steel but in some cases, for example, in Fig. 29:3, there were signs of a banded structure which probably indicates that the steel was originally in the form of a cast ingot and that the banding is due to phosphorus segregation upon solidification. But, of course, similar structures could be obtained by 'piling', that is, by welding laminations of thin steel like flaky pastry. In the post-medieval period this was known as 'shear steel'. Usually this technique results in slag inclusions along the line of the welds but if done extremely well it is possible to avoid these.

Knife blades

Fig. 29:14.   The structure of the blade is an example of shear steel like the modern scythe, in which the steel core is surrounded by wrought iron. The outer surfaces of the blade are ferrite with high ductility and low hardness, while the core and hence the projecting cutting edge is homogeneous carbon steel. This particular blade has not been heat-treated to put the core into its hardest state but the core has a ferrite and sorbitic-pearlite structure with a hardness of 239; the hardness of the ferritic surface is 92.

Fig. 29:1.   A better knife made by the 'steeling' process, in which ready-made carbon steel is welded on to the parts that need it, that is the cutting edges. In the seventeenth century this steel was usually a costly import from Sweden and Russia, and was therefore treated with great care. It certainly gives this impression here. This particular knife has been quenched after welding, from a temperature exceeding 800°C., and lightly tempered to give a hardness of 857. This is extremely well made and heat-treated and would presumably be used as a butcher's knife.

The majority of the Chingley knives were softer than 29:1. This was necessary as the homogeneous carbon steel from which they were made would have been too brittle in its fully hardened state.

Fig. 29:2. Homogeneous but rather low carbon steel decarburized at the surface. Hardness at the edge in low carbon area, 296; at the back it reaches 391 in the centre and 218 near the surface. The structure looks as though it may have been quenched between 700 and 800°C., that is, in the ferrite and austenite phase field, giving a ferrite and martensite structure with a maximum carbon content of about 0.5%. The bolster and tang seem to have been made by welding on a piece of wrought iron to the steel blade to thicken the back end, and then forging the two pieces together to give the thicker bolster and the thinner tang. The weld in the two pieces can be seen in the bolster (across the corners) and in the tang across the flats. The hardness of the wrought iron in the bolster is 135 HV1.

Knife Blanks

Fig. 29:5. Wrought iron with a hardness of 124 HV. Probably a blank for a steel-edged knife.

Five strips of iron and steel. The widest was a piece of fairly homogeneous steel made by piling and would have made a good knife. It now consists of tempered martensite with a hardness of 450. The rest are mostly pure iron and not one of them would make a good knife as they stand. In some, there were some laminations containing a little carbon. One was heavily piled with as much as 0.4% C. at one end (the thinner) in which the pearlite had been slightly spheroidized by long heating at 600–700°C. The other end had 0.3% C. which was more highly spheroidized. This could have made a reasonable knife if it had been quenched and tempered.

Fig. 29:13. Scythe Fragment. This is wrought iron of low carbon content. The rim has been formed by forging or upsetting the sheet. A very neat piece of work as it does not seem to have been bent round to thicken the rim. The piece may have started as a piece as thick as the rim, and the thin part forged down.

Scissors

The scissors are rather a mixed bag; some are pure ferrite with a hardness of 121 to 195, the latter due to high phosphorus. A good example of steeling is in the scissors 29:6, in which the blade is of fairly low-carbon steel with some slag, and the cutting edge sorbitic carbon steel. But the difference in the hardness is not very great (blade 182, edge 221), probably because the blade contains phosphorus which would harden it, while no heat-treatment has been given that would harden the carbon steel edge.

The scissors 29:8 have been made from shear steel and a very successful heat treatment operation has been carried out which has hardened the steel core to 549. The blade surface is ferritic with a hardness of 119; there is some diffusion of carbon from the steel. Scissors 29:9 are of the same type of steel and the steel core consists of tempered martensite with some slag and has a hardness of 460. The ferrite on the thicker side has a hardness of 139 and contains some pearlite.

The tang was examined to see whether this blade was formed from a re-used knife, as the sandwich structure resembled that from a knife rather than scissors. But the tang was mostly ferrite and showed no trace of a steel insert. The tip of the tang was ferritic with a hardness of 118, while further along there was some pearlite giving a hardness of 151. The carbon content varied from 0.0% to about 0.15%. The ferrite was mostly equiaxed with a little grain boundary carbide.

The area of the rivet was examined in the scissors 29:7. The rivet is ferritic with some grain boundary carbide but its hardness is 285–296 which is rather higher than one would expect and suggests some work-hardening. The hole in the blade has been drifted. The blade is ferrite with hardnesses of 121–130. There is no evidence of steeling in this part of the implement.

Conclusions   The knives and scissors show the use of techniques that had been developing since the early medieval period. Very little has been written on the techniques used in early cutlery — and it must be remembered that scissors as distinct from shears were a medieval invention — but we know that the use of steel was gradually replacing the Early Iron Age and Roman processes of local carburization (cementation) and the Anglo-Saxon and Early Medieval process of pattern welding.[1] Inserts of steel had been used on Viking-type axe-heads, and high quality arrow heads were steeled in the thirteenth century.[2]

In the more recent period (eighteenth–nineteenth centuries) more or less homogeneous steels were being used for cutlery. In these, the single shear or double shear process of piling blister steel bars was the main technique used. As far as the period that we are involved in here is concerned — the late seventeenth to the early eighteenth centuries — we have very little information and this collection is therefore of great value if only as a beginning. We see here a transition between the late medieval use of the sandwich type of construction for the knives and steeling for the scissors, and the more recent use of shear steel for knives.

It would appear that it was the general intention of the smith to make the knives of homogeneous shear steel and the scissors of steeled wrought iron. The latter would have been expected from the large amount of metal in the handle of the scissors which could have been quite adequately made in wrought iron. For this reason it would seem that the scissors blade 29:9 was intended originally as a knife; it certainly has a knife shape and is quite different from the more rounded shape of 29:6 which typifies the scissors. Likewise, the knife 29:1 is steeled and has a section much more like that of the scissors than the knives.

It is understandable that the steeling process should have a longer life in the case of the scissors; and naturally, the sandwich type of construction would be used in such a way as to leave a tang of wrought iron which could, if necessary, be formed into the handle of the scissors.

TOOLS

Fig. 30.   Five of the wedges, drifts or feathers were sectioned and all five were of wrought iron. They were made by piling techniques, and here and there were slight traces of carburization which were clearly unintentional. The hardness varied from 99–177HV. At the sharpened edge there was often a considerable amount of splaying along the slag lines indicating that a fair amount of force had been used. There is little doubt of this from the mushroomed head of some of the wedges.

From the five objects examined it is pretty clear that all these items are of common wrought iron and that as they exist none of them was intended as a tool, in the sense that none could have been used as a punch or a blacksmiths' drift since these would need steeling. I suspect that they have been used as wedges in a number of applications, perhaps in the water-wheels in the forge.

Fig. 31:54.   Drift, square in section, steeled by having a strip of carbon steel welded on to one side for the whole length of the drift so that it takes up most of the area of the point. The carbon content of the steel must be about 0.7–0.8%, and that in the body of the drift has a pearlitic structure with a hardness of 239. But at the point it has been quench-hardened to give a structure of martensite and troostite with a hardness of 726. The low carbon body of the

[1] B. A. Kolchin, 'Novgorod: A Metallurgical Examination of the Iron Artifacts', in Artsikhovsky and Kolchin (eds), *Works of the Novgorod Expedition: Materials and Researches on the Archaeology of the U.S.S.R.*, 65 (1959); J. Piaskowski, *Studia z dziejów górnictwa i hutnictwa* (1959), 3, 7–102; Materiały Muz. Arch. Etn. Lodz 7 (1962), 225–57; *Fonderia Italian*, 8, 269–81; *Jnl. Iron and Steel Inst.* 202 (1964), 561–8.
[2] Schubert 1957, p. 117.

drift had a ferrite + pearlite structure with a Widmanstätten distribution which shows that it has been heated at some time to a high temperature and cooled fairly fast, probably when the tip was hardened. This tool shows a good understanding of the technique of heat treatment and would have been a very useful tool for making the rivet holes in the scissors, for example.

Fig. 31:55. Drift, circular in section; wholly ferritic with a hardness of 154. The tip has not been hardened in any way.

Fig. 31:56. Drift, mushroom head deformed by hammering. A piece was taken from the head and found to be heavily deformed ferrite with a twinned structure and a hardness of 202–265. The material was 100% ferrite and the high hardness reflects the deformation. But in order to get deformation twins (Neumann lamellae) by hammering, the iron usually has to have a high phosphorus or nickel content.

Fig. 32:61. Axe. This is simple shear steel with a high carbon layer sandwiched between two layers of wrought iron. Marked arsenic banding is present at the welds and there is slight diffusion of carbon from the steel into the iron. The steel has a tempered martensite structure and a hardness of 391 HV at the cutting edge and 376 at the back. The iron sides have a hardness of about 175.

Fig. 32:63. Wood chisel with a socketed handle. This was found to have a steeled edge. Unless this tool had suffered considerable wear in use, which did not seem likely, the steel was again used very economically, so much so that the steeled length remaining was only 1.2 cm., and the steel itself limited to the cutting part of the blade. The edge consists of martensite and troostite showing that it had had a rather slower quench than the other hardened implements. This could have been done in oil or water; if the latter, no attempt had been made to 'stir' the end to get the maximum effect or else the water had been hot. The body of the chisel is ferrite with a hardness of 139.

The socket had been shaped into a hexagonal section by forming the socket in a manner rather like that of a spearhead.[1] This has resulted in a single weld line coinciding with one corner of the hexagon. The angles of the hexagon were very sharp showing that it had been hot forged on a very angular mandrel. The weld was almost invisible for half its length and the other half was marked by slag inclusions. One side of the join had a Widmanstätten structure showing that it had been carburized to some extent while heating, and had been fairly fast cooled after welding. Otherwise the metal was ferritic with a hardness of 113 which shows that the phosphorus was low.

Fig. 32:64. Tanged gouge. This was sectioned in the middle of its length, as any cutting edge seemed to have rusted away. This area was found to be ferrite and slag with a hardness of 112–113.

KEYS AND LOCKS

PERIOD I

Fig. 27:4. Key. Made from one piece of wrought iron; there are no signs of brazing or welding nor does it contain any steel.

PERIODS II AND III

Fig. 35:98. Padlock bolt. A section cut through the spines and leaf springs showed them all to be wrought iron, fairly pure and of low carbon content, with a hardness in the range 82–100 HV1. Some of the leaves have slightly carburized surfaces giving hardnesses in the range 135–165 HV1, but I think that the carburization here was accidental rather than intentional.

[1] R. Pleiner, *Stare Evropske Kovarstvi* (Prague, 1962), p. 22.

Fig. 35:103. Padlock. The spring is of spring steel hardened to 401–480 HV — tempered martensite; the hasp is basically merely fine-grained ferrite with a little pearlite near the surface (0.1–0.2% C.) but the hardness of 165 HV1 suggests a fairly high phosphorus or some cold work.

 Case and binding. The remains of the case have a hardness of 205–210 HV1 and are again wrought iron with high phosphorus and some cold work. The binding is certainly a brass. The structure consists of single phase equiaxed grains with slight residual coring with marked slip marking but with complete absence of any twinning. The hardness is 102 HV1. These features are more characteristic of a beta brass than alpha which suggests a zinc content of 40%. The brass is well bonded to the steel and would appear to have been applied in the molten state either as a strip or melted-on droplets. After application it has been finally planished with a hammer. It is certainly not a case of hammer welding.

SPUR

Fig. 36:120. Rowel Spur. This was sectioned down the neck to see whether this had been welded on, but it is clear that it has been made out of one piece of wrought iron. It is possible that the neck has been carburized, as there are slight traces of grain boundary carbide near the end; but most of the neck has rusted away. There are traces of pearlite in the part near the heel, and the hardness varies between 113 and 117 showing that this item has a low phosphorus content.

WEAPONS AND FIREARMS

Fig. 37:123. Pommel. At first sight this looked like a cored iron casting. A small piece removed from the base showed quite clearly that it is made of wrought iron. The structure is almost pure ferrite with slag inclusions and heavy twinning which shows that this part had had severe cold work. The hardness was 193 which suggests that we are dealing with a fairly pure phosphorus-free iron which could be easily forged and engraved.

 This pommel had been made by hot forging a small bloom over a stake anvil, like those used for helmets and shield bosses, so that one gets a closed-ended tube. The open end is then partially closed by swaging down round the collar just short of the end. The slag stringers show this quite clearly as they are at right angles to the direction of the section. After forging down to the right shape, the holes were put in by drilling or drifting and the design carefully engraved. A number of these pommels are shown in *Made of Iron*, a catalogue of an exhibition of artistic iron objects.[1] These are all made from wrought iron and seem to be of French origin; but it is possible that the idea was copied in England.

Fig. 38:124. Pommel. This had been made from a single piece of wrought iron. It has a hole through it and the tang of the sword has been passed through this hole and riveted over on the top. There were no traces of any brazing or soldering medium and the joint was purely mechanical. It seems however, that the overall surface has been plated; if so, this was certainly not copper-based material but it could have been tin or lead-tin.

Fig. 38:131. Grenade(?) Made of wrought iron with about 0.1% C. The carbon is in the form of very coarse almost spheroidal pearlite and it would seem to have been heated for a long time at about 600–700°C. There is marked penetration of a copper-base alloy, probably brass, which suggests that the two halves have been brazed together. The hardness of the iron is 135 HV5 and that of the brazing metal is not very much less.

 The contents are now mostly hydrated iron oxide (yellow ochre) in granular form which turns a good red (hematite) on heating. There is a little charcoal present but no sulphur.

---

[1] *Made of Iron*, A catalogue of an exhibition held at Houston, Texas, 1966, p. 217.

It could have contained a filling consisting of iron filings or iron scale with a little charcoal and perhaps sodium nitrate — the latter having been dissolved away by surface water. Biringuccio mentions both iron filings and iron scale as fillings for fire bombs etc. Iron filings are one of the constituents of modern fireworks such as sparklers. On the other hand, the iron oxide could merely be a deposit from iron-bearing waters, and thus the object cannot be definitely shown to have contained an explosive.

Fig. 38:132. Gun-lock. Both springs are made of tempered martensite. The main spring is homogeneous, with a hardness of 378 HV1. The sear spring is thinner, piled, and more variable in composition with arsenic enrichment bands. Again it is tempered martensite with a hardness of 467 HV1. The hardness on the surface of the boss round the hole was in the range 237–299 HV5, which tends to suggest that the body of the lock was unhardened 0.8% carbon steel.

Box Iron

136. *Not illustrated.* This consists of brazed wrought iron. The strengthening-ribs of the base have been brazed to the sole-plate and the sole-plate has been bent over near the back edge and has been penetrated by brazing metal. The brass has the mottled appearance of a cored cast metal and some traces of a compound. The dark areas are intergranular shrinkage cavities. The brazing appears to have been well-done under reducing conditions and followed by slow cooling. The hardness of the braze was 75 HV1 and the zinc content of the brass must be near the solubility limit of 30%. It is perhaps worth mentioning that one of the things that Isaac Wilkinson was casting at Backbarrow in 1738 was said to be smoothing irons.[1] Presumably the Chingley example represents the method of construction used previously.

Cast Iron

128. *Not illustrated.* One-pound cannon ball of white iron with a hardness of 343–393. This is a very good casting with little porosity and a low phosphorus content, but it has quite a lot of sulphur present as manganese sulphide. It would seem that this was probably not made from local nodular ore, which contains 0.65% P_2O_5 (at Ashburnham).[2] This is a very good example of casting and shows that the alleged low quality cast iron balls of Armada vintage were quite unnecessarily poor. The toughness of this specimen was a surprise to the present author and will cause him to revise some of his ideas about the brittleness of white cast iron.

Fig. 44:10. Cast iron cauldron; very hard, white cast iron with slight graphitization. Hardness 700 HV5. Typical of low silicon, charcoal iron. (Furnace.)

Fig. 40:148. Cauldron leg. A chilled white iron on the outside and a grey iron on the inside. This is quite normal for a cast iron with low silicon content, particularly from early cold-blast charcoal-fuelled furnaces. The rate of cooling in the clay-sand mould is too fast to get the normal grey iron throughout and the outside surfaces solidifies as 'white' cast iron. Corrosion has detached the 'white' from the 'grey' because of their markedly different properties. The iron is quite high in phosphorus, with graphite and pearlite on the inside.

Miscellaneous Objects

Fig. 41:152. Wrought iron tube with a blob of brass adhering to its outer surface. The tube has a hardness of 127–144 which is due to the presence of some pearlite. One would think that the brass was intended to join the edges of the strip together to form the tube but no brass seems to have penetrated the gap. The structure of the brass is equiaxed but shows little sign of working, except on the surface, and no coring. It therefore seems that it was cast on to the

---

[1] A. Fell, *The Early Iron Industry of Furness and District* (Ulverston, 1908), p. 240.
[2] Tylecote 1962, p. 180.

surface of the iron and subsequently heated below its melting point for some time. It is a single-phase alloy and has a hardness of 103 which would suggest that it is an alpha brass (70 Cu/30 Zn) with some soluble impurities. The zinc content might be as high as 35%.

A section was removed from half-way along the length of the tube to see if the 'braze' was more effective than it was near the blob of brass. But there was no brass visible, and the tube had not been closed in any way. Its structure is essentially ferritic with a hardness of 186 although there is a small amount of pearlite in some places. Also, the inside of the tube has suffered some carburization giving as much as 0.4%C. in one place and a Widmanstätten structure. It would appear that this tube was a failure and therefore rejected.

Fig. 41:156. Nut, sectioned through the screw threads. Although screw threads have been known since Roman times, the early ones are usually made of wood. After medieval times metal screws became quite common and various authors such as Burstall[1] show the way that they were made. In this case the nut was ferritic with a hardness of 137 and the threads had been cut with a blunt tool using considerable force so that there is much evidence of cold work. The thread contour is not very even but this is more likely to be due to rusting.

Fig. 41:157. Wrought iron with a hardness of 199.

NON-FERROUS OBJECTS

PERIOD I

Fig. 28:1–2, 4. Two strap-end buckles and one strap end; these objects were of wrought, annealed and reworked material mostly probably brass sheet with a hardness of 133 HV1. The plates of 28:1 had been wetted on one surface with liquid metal, probably lead-tin solder which had resulted in intergranular penetration and subsequent cracking which is not un-expected for a cold-worked brass. These must have been soldered as well as riveted to the narrower parts projecting from the frame of the buckle.

A piece of bronze from 28:4 showed considerable delta phase but some signs of solution treatment. The hardness was only 87 HV1 showing that there was little remaining cold work. The remaining two pieces (28:2) were also bronze, but fully solid solution with no trace of the delta phase; one had been wrought and annealed and then heavily cold-worked while the other seemed to lack the final cold work.

It seems that the buckles were made from bronze castings finally worked by hammering and then finished by soldering and riveting on brass side plates.

From the same deposit, there were mixed pieces of copper-base alloy, mostly offcuts from strip or sheet. All are worked and annealed and some of them have been cold worked. They are all solid solution material showing no signs of a delta phase. They could be brass or bronze but the colouring shows that the majority are brass with one or two pieces of gilding metal or tin-bronze. The hardnesses varied from 77 through 89 and 108 to 125. The bronze-looking piece had a hardness of 108 (all HV1). All the metal is very clean with little slag or oxide.

Fig. 28:7. Bronze cauldron leg. Porous and very leaded cast bronze somewhat corroded. The tin content must be fairly high (over 10%) as it contains a lot of the delta eutectoid. The hardness varies from 70–86 HV1. The lead content is in the range 10–20%.

8. *Not illustrated.* The spherical piece is a bronze casting with a very little lead and a good deal of delta. It is a good, sound, casting with no corrosion and non-porous. The hardness is in the range 72–87 HV1.

---

[1] A. F. Burstall, *A History of Engineering* (London, 1963), pp. 78, 125.

PERIODS II AND III

15. *Not illustrated*. Either gate (waste metal from casting) or rivet. A cast copper-base solid solution with a considerable amount of deformation. The hardness is 108 HV2.5. There is some small amount of a second phase, probably oxide or sulphide. Probably an impure cast copper, formed into its present shape largely by cold hammering.

PINS

PERIOD I

5a. *Not illustrated*. The pin is hard drawn brass wire with a brass head soldered on. There is some trace of a flux at the edge suggesting that the soldering was done with the aid of a viscous flux. The solder is a lot softer than the brass and may be of the lead-tin type or one more complex containing zinc. Hardness of shank, 189; head 121 HV1.

PERIOD III

3. *Not illustrated*. This pin was of drawn brass wire and had a hardness of 168 near the head and 120 near the tip. It would appear to be a 70/30 brass with elongated grey inclusions of (?)zinc oxide. The head was quite unlike the previous specimen and was soldered with a lead-tin solder. It was made from a two-turn spiral of brass wire — a technique well known in the eighteenth century and described by Diderot[1] and Hamilton.[2] There was no tapering of the head-end of the shank and no effort had been made to form a globular head. The resulting head was much more cylindrical than no. 4. There was slight dezincification of one of the two components of the head which must have occurred during annealing.

By 1762, pin-heads were being made by upsetting spirals of drawn wire as is clearly shown by Diderot. Hamilton notes that this method of making pin heads was still in use in Birmingham around 1810. It is probable that pin 3 is an exceptional case of local manufacture. We certainly need more information on the techniques of pin making before the eighteenth century.

4. *Not illustrated*. A gilded brass pin which was found to have a most interesting structure. It has been made from three pieces of 70/30 brass in the worked and annealed condition with hardnesses in the range 73–80. The shank has been pointed and has had brazed on to it a piece of sheet which has been bent over. On to this was brazed another piece of similar sheet also bent over and carefully rounded to complete the round head. The brazing metal was coppery in colour but was clearly not brass: its melting point would have been too high. An electron microprobe examination showed that it contained copper and sulphur. It therefore seems to be one of the niello-type materials; but to have a melting point below that of brass it would have to be complex and therefore it probably contains silver and lead sulphides as well; it certainly had good fluidity as it has flowed into a crack in the shank of the pin.[3]

---

[1] D. Diderot and J. D'Alembert, *Encyclopedie . . . des Arts et des Metiers* (Paris, 1751–77). v, 804–7.
[2] H. Hamilton, *History of the English Brass and Copper Industries* (London, 1936), pp. 256–7.
[3] R. F. Tylecote, 'A Contribution to the Metallurgy of 18th and 19th-century Brass Pins', *Post-Medieval Archaeology*, 6 (1972), 183–90. The microprobe examination was undertaken by Dr C. W. Haworth, Department of Metallurgy, University of Sheffield.

Select Bibliography

Agricola, G.	*De Re Metallica*, Basle 1556; edited by H. and L. Hoover, New York, 1950.
Biringuccio, V.	*Pirotechnia*, Venice 1540–1549; translated by C. S. Smith and M. T. Gnudi, New York, 1942.
Cattell, C. S.	'An Evaluation of the Loseley List of Ironworks within the Weald in the year 1588', *Archaeologia Cantiana*, 86 (1971), 85–92.
Crossley, D. W., and Ashurst, D.	'Excavations at Rockley Smithies, a water-powered Bloomery of the 16th and 17th Centuries', *Post-Medieval Archaeology*, 2 (1968), 10–54.
Crossley, D. W.	'A 16th-century Wealden Blast Furnace: a report on Excavations at Panningridge, Sussex, 1964–1970', *Post-Medieval Archaeology*, 6 (1972), 42–68.
Hulme, E. W.	'Statistical History of the Iron Trade of England and Wales', *Trans. Newcomen Society*, 9 (1928–9), 12–35.
Money, J. H.	'Medieval Iron-workings in Minepit Wood, Rotherfield, Sussex', *Medieval Archaeology*, 15 (1971), 86–111.
Parsons, J. L.	'The Sussex Ironworks', *Sussex Archaeological Collections*, 32 (1882), 19–32.
Schubert, H. R.	'The Early Refining of Pig Iron in England', *Trans. Newcomen Society*, 28 (1951–3), 59–75.
Schubert, H. R.	*History of the British Iron and Steel Industry from c. 450 B.C. to A.D. 1775*, London, 1957.
Shepherd-Thorn, E. R. and others.	*Geology of the Country round Tenterden*, London, 1966.
Straker, E.	*Wealden Iron*, London, 1931, repr. Newton Abbot, 1969.
Tylecote, R. F.	*Metallurgy in Archaeology*, London, 1962.

PLATE I

The Forge Period I. Timber structures from the south-east. Scale: 1 metre

PLATE II

B. The Forge   Period II.   Centre long member
overlying cut-down vertical of Period I.
Scale divisions: 20 cm.

A. The Forge   Period I.   Top joint, south-east corner.
Scale divisions: 20 cm.

PLATE III

A. The Forge   Period I.   Intermediate verticals east side, south bay,
Scale: 1 metre

B. The Forge   Period I.   Base frame: dovetail joint (U–V).
For dimensions see Appendix, p. 37

PLATE IV

The Forge   Period I.   Base frame: tenon joint (u–s).   Scale divisions: 20 cm.

PLATE V

A. The Forge   Period I.   (left middle-ground) beneath II (centre), beneath sleeper of III (long member across foreground).   Scale: 2 metres

B. The Forge   Period II.   West side of wheel-pit, with Period III sleepers in the foreground.   Scale: 1 metre

PLATE VI

The Forge   Period II. South end, from the west.   Scale: 1 metre

PLATE VII

The Forge Period III. Finery building and race. Scale: 2 metres

PLATE VIII

A. The Forge   Period IIIA.   Hammer fulcrum post.   Scale: 3 ft

B. The Forge   Period IIIB.   Breast-wheel pit for hammer, with chafery hearth
fragment in the foreground.   Scale: 3 ft

PLATE IX

The Forge   Period IIIB.   The southern end of the breast-wheel pit, with cut-through
Period II timbers (background).   Scale: 1 metre

PLATE X

A. The Forge Period IIIB. Anvil, with radial supports in position. Scale: 3 ft

B. The Forge Period IIIB. Anvil pit, partly excavated, with some radials removed and base foundation exposed. Scales: 3 ft

PLATE XI

A. The Forge   Period IIIB.   Base for small anvil, placed over filling covering Period II wheel-pit, and western sill beam of forge building.   Scale: 1 metre

B. The Forge   Period IIIB.   Chafery wheel-pit, from the east.   Scale: 1 metre

PLATE XII

The Furnace Overall, from the south. Scale: 1 metre

PLATE XIII

The Furnace   The hearth.   Scale: 1 metre

PLATE XIV

The Furnace   The wheel, in course of excavation.   Scale: 1 metre

PLATE XV

The Furnace   The wheel-pit, after removal of the wheel, from the tailrace.
Scale divisions: 20 cm.

PLATE XVI

The Furnace   The bellows supports from the south-east.   Scale: 1 metre